COMFORT FOOD MAKEOVERS

COMFORT FOOD MAKEOVERS

Healthy Alternatives to Your Favorite Homestyle Dishes

By Elaine Magee, MPH, RD

Black Dog & Leventhal
Paperbacks

Published by
Black Dog & Leventhal Publishers
151 W. 19th Street
New York, NY 10011

Distributed by Workman Publishing Company
708 Broadway
New York, NY 10003

Manufactured in China

Cover and interior design by Kay Schuckhart, Blonde on Pond Design

Cover photographs courtesy of Getty Images/Burke/Triolo Productions and Foodpix/Picture Arts

ISBN: 1-57912-464-X

g f e d c b a

Library of Congress Cataloging-in-Publication Data

Magee, Elaine.
    Comfort food makeovers : healthy alternatives to your favorite homestyle dishes / by Elaine Magee.
      p. cm.
    ISBN: 1-57912-464-X
    1. Cookery. I. Title.

TX714.M33655 2006
614.5--dc22   2005048338

Dedication

This book is dedicated with love and gratitude to Troy Spencer
(our favorite 7th grade science teacher). In Troy's honor, 10% of the royalties for
this book will be given to the American Cancer Society.

CONTENTS

CHAPTER ONE

Feel-Good Foods

Piping-hot macaroni and cheese with a crunchy golden-brown crust, chewy and gooey chocolate chip cookies warm from the oven, or a big mound of fluffy white mashed potatoes with a pool of melted butter dripping down the side: Who doesn't like comfort food?

Running through a quick list of comfort foods in your mind, you might notice that they usually have an appealing texture and "mouth feel," and a rich and creamy quality that encourages that secure, full feeling in your stomach. Just biting into a favorite comfort food takes you back to a time when you felt happy and nourished, loved and cared for. It's hard to argue with that kind of power.

In life's trials and tribulations and even in its little celebrations along the way, we reach for our favorite comfort foods. We just can't help it. We all need a little extra comfort every now and then. But with the stressful lives we lead these days, we want our comfort foods more often than ever before. According to a recent survey commissioned by the American Institute for Cancer Research, 57 million Americans reported that they are currently eating more comfort foods—meatloaf, fried chicken, and chocolate cake—than ever. "When we are anxious or fearful, we fall back to foods we associate with times of lowest stress—that is, with childhood," says Dr. John Foreyt of the Behavioral Medicine Center at Baylor College of Medicine. This is what comfort food is all about. Eating the food today helps conjure up memories and feelings associated with eating that food long ago. Comfort foods are *feel-good* foods, soothing and nurturing us, but they usually come with a rather steep nutritional price tag: Comfort foods are generally high in fat and calories, and sometimes even in sugar. Remember, many comfort foods became staples on our dinner tables at a time when Americans actually needed calorie-dense meals to keep up with their physically demanding jobs. But this was before Americans became more stagnant, and before it became well known that the food we eat directly influences our health.

Should We Give Up Our Comfort Foods?

Is the answer to resist comforting ourselves with these foods that we crave? "I do not believe we should deny ourselves these foods which we have emotional attachments to," assures Rebecca Reeves, an obesity researcher at Baylor College. "If we do deprive ourselves, we'll just want to eat more and more." Reeves suggests that we indulge in our comfort foods but urges us to use moderation, especially if these foods are high in calories and fat.

EMOTIONAL EATERS: WHO IS AT RISK?

Take a good look at your self-esteem, whether the people around you support you, and whether your basic needs are being met. These are just three of the factors that help predict who is vulnerable to emotional eating (eating in response to emotions) and who is not.

• Do You Have Emotional Support in Your Life?
According to a recent study in *Preventive Medicine* (January 2002), women who report that they receive no or very little emotional support from their spouse, close friends, and relatives are more likely to engage in stress-related eating and drinking. This tells us that any weight-loss program that women participate in should cover the way we deal with emotions and give us ways to improve the emotional support in our lives.

• Have You Checked Your Self-Esteem Lately?

In another study in *Issues in Mental Health Nursing* (October/November 2001), researchers found that the less satisfied women were that their basic needs were being met, the more likely they were to engage in emotional eating. "Low satisfaction with meeting self-esteem needs was the strongest predictor of emotional eating," says Gayle Timmerman, an author of the study and an associate professor at the University of Texas at Austin School of Nursing. This suggests that working on building self-esteem can serve as an internal resource for women, helping us to continue to practice healthier behaviors by dealing with the stress in our lives without resorting to emotional eating.

• Don't Be So Negative!
When women rated their momentary emotional states and their motivation to eat for six days, researchers discovered that during periods of negative emotions there was a heightened tendency to cope through eating. Women also reported more intense hunger sensations during these periods.

Can any good come from eating comfort foods? You bet! There are at least two ways in which comfort foods can physically help your body. Many of the most popular comfort foods actually offer significant nutritional value, especially when they've been made over to be lower in fat and sugar calories and higher in fiber and other important nutrients. Healthful comfort food options include breads and stews and vegetable-containing casseroles in particular. Also, in the first animal data of its kind, we now have evidence that eating comfort foods may even be good for us, because they function as stress reducers. When Mary Dallman, the chief investigator of a University of California San Francisco study, subjected rats to chronic stress over a few days, she discovered that they preferred to eat sugar and fat. Who knew that rats would want to eat the same types of foods when they're stressed out as we do! And when the rats satisfied their desire by eating sugar and fat, their brains produced less of the stress-related hormones (the ones that traditionally trigger the fight-or-flight response). This suggests that in times of stress rats (and probably humans) tend to reach for foods that are high in fat and sugar, and that eating these types of foods may reduce the amount of stress hormones the brain produces in response to the stress.

Which Comfort Foods Top the Charts?

Take a guess at what some of the top comfort foods are. Depending on your generation, the part of the country you grew up in, and your ethnicity, the list of favorite comfort foods will shift a bit. Macaroni and cheese and chocolate chip cookies are probably in there somewhere, right? But what are the Top 20 comfort foods that people around the country crave? Well, apparently the answer can depend on whether you're male or female.

While men seem to prefer warm, hearty meat-related comfort foods, such as steak, casseroles, and soup, women prefer more snack-related foods like chocolate or ice cream, according to a recent University of Illinois study. No matter what your comfort food preferences are, there's something for everyone in *Comfort Food Makeovers*—from chocolate brownies, cookies, cakes, and ice cream to marinated flank steak, contemporary casseroles, and soups, stews, and chili. All the comfort food bases are covered!

To be doubly sure that we included recipe "makeovers" of all the top comfort foods, one of the largest recipe Web sites, www.allrecipes.com, invited its members to select their top three favorite comfort foods. More than 6,400 people took the survey, and the survey says that these are the top comfort foods in America:

FAVORITE COMFORT FOODS

Ranking	Food	% of Members Selecting It
1	Mashed potatoes and gravy	48%
2	Macaroni and cheese	34%
3	Chocolate chip cookies	30% (tied with No. 4)
4	Ice cream	30%
5	Soup	28%
6	Pizza	27%
7	Pot roast	25%
8	Fried chicken	24%
9	Pasta	23% (tied with No. 10)
10	Grilled cheese	23%
11	Meatloaf	22%
12	Brownies	20%
13	Apple pie	18%
14	Chocolate cake	17% (tied with Nos. 15–17)
15	French fries	17%
16	Biscuits	17%
17	Lasagna	17%
18	Stew	16%
19	Hamburger	15%
20	Potato chips	14%

Which of these Top 20 comfort foods are the worst offenders if you're trying to trim down? It's much easier to ask which ones *are not* high in fat and calories. There are only three comfort foods on this list that won't send your calorie budget into overdrive: soup, pot roast, and stew. The good news is, of the remaining seventeen comfort foods, you can make smarter choices with all of them and still maintain the same flavor and texture that made them so satisfying to begin with. There are no lost causes in this Top 20 list.

THE OTHER COMFORT FAVORITES

There were a lot more than twenty comfort foods mentioned in the vote. Here are some that had plenty of votes but didn't rank in the Top 20:

Chocolate *

Chicken and dumplings *

Fresh baked bread *

Chili *

Cheesecake *

Steak *

Eggs *

Roasted turkey with gravy and stuffing *

Pecan pie *

Chicken fried steak

Baked potatoes

Spaghetti *

Tapioca pudding *

Pork chops

Potato salad *

Chicken and noodles *

Tacos *

Chicken pot pie *

Roast chicken *

Bread pudding *

Peach cobbler *

Biscuits and gravy *

Pasta *

Sheperd's pie *

Cinnamon rolls *

Apple crisp *

Cherry pie *

Coconut cream pie *

Corn bread *

If the food has a * next to it, we've included at least one light recipe that is similar to this dish in *Comfort Food Makeovers.*

Ten Ways to Have Your Comfort Foods and Eat Light, Too

Many of us enjoy our favorite comfort foods in large portion sizes, possibly because when we eat them we are in an overindulging or emotional-eating mode. Traveling down this road can lead to eating even more calories than we care to consume. To make matters worse, many of the types of comfort foods we crave tend to be particularly dense in fat and sugar calories and low in nutritional value, making the extra calories add up pretty quickly. This begs the question: How do we comfort ourselves without consuming all those extra calories and fat? Here are ten tips to help you do just that!

1. Eat your comfort food when you are truly hungry; trust me, you'll enjoy it even more and it will taste even better. This way, the comfort food will satisfy your physical hunger and nourish your body at the same time. According to a recent study, almost half the time people eat something to satisfy a craving, they're not actually hungry.

2. Know your comfort food craving triggers! What makes you crave, seek out, and possibly overeat comfort foods? Identifying a problem is said to be 90 percent of the solution. But when it comes to food issues, that last 10 percent can be a doozie.

   The following are some possible triggers. Think about which ones hit home for you:
   - **Stress**
   - **Boredom**
   - **Habit**
   - **Anxiety and worry**
   - **Pain**
   - **Disappointment or rejection**
   - **Happiness and celebration**
   - **Depression**
   - **Other triggers**

3. Stop eating your comfort food when you're comfortable—not when you're "full." Some of us have a tendency to overeat our favorite comfort foods (partly because they taste so darn good). Pay close attention to how your stomach feels while you're eating, and if you eat slowly and really savor your meal or snack, it might be easier to sense when your stomach is comfortable and not full or stuffed.

4. Set yourself up for comfort food success. Ideally, you want to enjoy your comfort food as part of your regular meal and not as an impulse snack, lessening the likelihood that you're eating for emotional reasons.

5. Whenever possible, prepare your comfort foods with recipes that have been given a nutritional "tune-up" and are lower in calories and fat as well as sodium and sugar. (You've already got this one licked, because you have *Comfort Food Makeovers* in hand!)

6. Don't deny yourself carbohydrates! It's no surprise that most of our top comfort foods contain an overload of carbs, because carbs help us feel good in the short and the long term. Within an hour or so after we eat carbohydrates, we get a boost in our levels of serotonin, which is the brain chemical that helps us feel calm and uplifted. And many of our favorite comfort foods offer plenty of fat grams to go with those carbs, too. But get this: High amounts of fat in food are also thought to create pleasurable sensations and lessen pain. The trick to lightening

comfort foods (and still have them taste great) is to cut the fat, calories, sugar, and sodium but not to take them out completely. You want to still have some of what makes the comfort food look and taste comforting and appealing, of course!

7. Don't ban comfort foods. This isn't the answer, because for most of us restricting foods can trigger even stronger cravings. It may take only a small serving to satisfy you. And if you're cooking up a light version of your favorite food, well, that's even better.

8. Drink more water and less caffeine. Caffeine and its dehydrating effects may help stimulate cravings for sweets. Don't overdo diet sodas either. Too much artificial sweetener may make you crave more sugar.

9. Trade instant gratification for sustained satisfaction. When it comes to comfort foods, we want instant gratification. We want our comfort food, and we want it now. But anything good is worth waiting for. Wait until you're truly hungry to enjoy your comfort food. Wait until you get the opportunity to prepare it at home, using a lower-calorie and lower-fat recipe. An even better idea is to boost the fiber in certain recipes and use less sugar. The meal will be more likely to encourage even blood sugars and energy levels for longer periods afterward.

10. Include small amounts of the comfort foods you crave—using lighter renditions whenever possible—in your normal healthful diet. Your cravings may be less severe and occur less often if you automatically incorporate more healthful versions of your favorite comfort foods into your weekly eating plan.

Keep the Comfort, Lose the Extra Calories

While many of us may applaud the pleasure principle exhibited in many of the comfort foods selected, the bottom line is that Americans are in a health crisis. Type 2 diabetes has reached epidemic proportions, and obesity has never been more prevalent. But Americans still want to eat the comfort foods they crave—the foods that make them feel good—while still keeping their calories and fat grams in check. Why spend 600 calories and 30 grams of fat on an entrée that will taste just as good and be just as satisfying with 400 calories and 13 grams of fat?

Obesity researcher Rebecca Reeves agrees. "If you can modify comfort foods for fat and calories and still have them taste delicious, then you can enjoy them even more," she says.

But can we truly satisfy our desire for comfort foods without going way over budget in the calorie and fat columns? You bet. With a few tried-and-true kitchen tricks, most com-

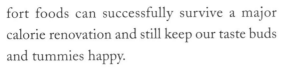

fort foods can successfully survive a major calorie renovation and still keep our taste buds and tummies happy.

When lightening up your favorite comfort foods, consider the three R's:

- Reduce the amount of high-fat/high-sugar/high-calorie ingredients in the recipe. And don't forget to reduce your portion size, too, especially if you tend to eat large servings.

- Replace the high-fat/high-sugar/high-sodium ingredients with reduced-fat, reduced-sugar, or reduced-sodium ingredients.

- Remove some high-fat, high-sugar ingredients that are not really necessary to carry out the recipe.

Keeping the three R's in mind, we've taken the top comfort foods and transformed them into equally comforting dishes, but always lower in calories and fat and sometimes also lower in sugar and sodium (see the "before" and "after" nutritional analysis for every recipe). Whether your favorite comfort food is meatloaf and mashed potatoes, chocolate chip cookies, or fried chicken, there is a lighter, flavorful version to behold. Here are some of the comfort food cooking tips I used while lightening the recipes in this book:

- Start with lean meat. Remove the skin and any visible fat.

- Reduce the amount of meat in the recipe and increase the amount of vegetables and beans (if possible). Sometimes you can use less meat than the recipe calls for and then increase the amount of vegetables by adding a second vegetable to the mix.

- There's no need to use lots of fat to brown the meat or sauté the vegetables. A little will usually do the trick—2 to 3 teaspoons [28 to 42 g] for a large skillet. Sometimes even a generous coating of canola oil cooking spray is enough.

- When a recipe calls for cream, use fat-free half-and-half, whole milk, or low-fat milk. Even a mixture of real half-and-half and low-fat milk will bring down the calories and fat in a big way when compared with using cream.

- Pass the reduced-fat cheese, please. There are some great-tasting reduced-fat cheeses that can be used in place of the regular cheese called for in a recipe without a big change in taste or texture. Reduced-fat cheeses usually have around 5 to 6 grams of fat per ounce compared with regular cheese, which has about 9 grams.

- If you want to cut the sugar calories in half, you have two options. You can simply add half the amount of sugar or sweetener called for (but if it's a liquid sweetener you'll have to compensate for the lost moisture). Or, if the idea of using an artificial sweetener interests you, you can use half the amount of sugar called for and make up the difference with Splenda. So far, this has worked out well for me when I bake and want to cut the sugar calories in half.

CALORIES STILL COUNT

When it comes to weight management, the rule of thumb isn't some magical protein versus carbohydrate formula. What is important is the total calories earned and the total calories spent. Obesity became the epidemic it is today at the same time daily calorie intake increased for the average American, at the same time portion sizes grew, and at the same time people became less physically fit.

Preparation Tips for the Top 10 Comfort Foods

Here are some tips to keep in mind before eating your favorite comfort foods:

Comfort Food	Shopping Tip
1. Mashed potatoes and gravy	If you know you'll want that pat of butter melting on top of your mound of mashed potatoes, be sure to add less or no butter when you're making the mashed potatoes themselves.
2. Macaroni and cheese	If you like the type of macaroni and cheese that comes in the box, don't worry. Just make it with 2 tablespoons [28 g] of butter instead of 4 [60 g] (and follow the rest of the directions on the box).

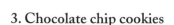

3. Chocolate chip cookies

If you cut the fat too much in your chocolate chip cookie recipe, it won't be a cookie anymore; it'll be a chocolate chip muffin. You can substitute shortening with light or fat-free cream cheese for one-third to one -half of the butter. If you like to buy your chocolate chip cookies in the grocery store, there are several tasty reduced-fat chocolate chip cookie brands on the market.

4. Ice cream

There are some really creamy and flavorful light ice creams on the market. Make sure your ice cream contains 3 or 4 grams of fat per ½ cup [66 g] serving. This way, it's lower in fat and calories but still tastes satisfying.

5. Soup

Clear broth and tomato-based soups are usually low in fat. But if you're buying your soups at the grocery store, check the calories and grams of fat on the nutrition label to make sure.

6. Pizza

If you're ordering your pizza from a restaurant, your best bet is not to go for the extra cheese or the fatty meats and to top your pizza with veggies instead. Eat your pizza with a salad or soup, so you won't be filling up on the bread alone.

7. Pot roast

Trim your pot roast of any visible fat before you cook it, and try not to add too much fat to the pan while preparing it. Keep it lean.

8. Fried chicken

You can still have the crispy brown breading on the outside and the moist, juicy chicken on the inside; you just have to oven-fry your chicken with a thin layer of canola oil cooking spray or a little oil on the breading. Remove the skin from the chicken breast before you put the coating on.

9. Pasta

Pasta itself isn't high in fat; it's what we pour on it that gets us into trouble. You can make lower-fat and lower-calorie creamy sauces by using less butter and switching to whole milk or fat-free half-and-half instead of cream. If you're going to use a fat in your pasta sauce, use olive or canola oil, and you can usually use less than the recipe calls for, too.

10. Grilled cheese

A lower-fat and lower-calorie grilled cheese sandwich is a nonstick skillet away. Coat your bread with a spray of canola oil cooking spray (or a thin coating of no-trans-margarine) and fill the bread with your favorite reduced-fat cheese.

Calling All Chocoholics!

Is chocolate the answer to bad moods, high stress, or broken hearts? Maybe not, but lots of people feel that it comes darn close. Life without chocolate would be a pretty tasteless place. I personally don't let a day go by without having a little bite of chocolate.

Chocolate is the Superman of all food cravings. Sixty-eight percent of women's food cravings are for chocolate. I can tell you that I for one am somewhere in that statistic. And at what time do we crave it the most? Apparently, chocolate is an afternoon delight.

A recent article in the *Journal of the American Dietetic Association* surmised that "chocolate cravings are real." Any woman could have told them that! And banning chocolate isn't such a good way to handle these very real cravings. A recent study on women of normal weight in the *International Journal of Eating Disorders* suggested that forbidding chocolate only leads to greater temptation and greater intake compared with women who have not been subjected to any special intervention.

A Little Goes a Long Way

It takes only six Hershey's kisses (about 1.5 ounces [42.5g] of chocolate) to give you a mild mood boost, according to food/mood researcher Laura Calderon, an associate professor at California State University.

For many, "comfort" is synonymous with "chocolate." What are some of the top-rated comfort foods? Try chocolate cookies, chocolate cake, brownies, and chocolate ice cream. No other food tantalizes the taste buds quite like chocolate—it represents a divine blend of more than 500 flavors (two-and-a-half times more flavors than any other food!). No other food has the sensual depth that chocolate does—even its melting point is sensual. Chocolate melts almost immediately in response to human touch because its melting point is just below body temperature. Couple that with its other appealing characteristics, such as the blend of fat and sugar, the smooth texture, and arousing aroma, and you've got—quite possibly—the most alluring food on the planet. But the appeal of chocolate isn't purely physical.

Part of what makes chocolate so desirable could be chemical. There may be a hormonal link to our chocolate cravings. Chocolate cravings often come and go with the monthly hormonal fluctuations and mood swings of women. There also happen to be several biologically active substances in chocolate (methylxanthines, biogenic amines, cannabi-noid-like fatty acids) that may cause psychological sensations similar to other addictive substances, according to the article in the *Journal of the American Dietetic Association.*

Here's the best news of all: Cocoa, the main ingredient in chocolate, may actually be good for you. In a recent study of antioxidants, cocoa was found to have the highest level of activity, beating out red wine, green tea, and black tea. Researchers also noted that cocoa had much higher levels of two phytochemicals

EAT MORE CHOCOLATE

The benefits of chocolate include the following:

- Chocolate provides us with a carbohydrate lift.

- Chocolate makes us feel good through chemicals like phenylethylamine, which triggers the release of endorphins (morphine-like chemicals in the body).

- Chocolate also contains other biologically active constituents (methylxanthines, biogenic amines, and cannabinoid-like fatty acids) that could potentially affect behavior in a positive way.

(total phenolics and flavonoids), per serving, compared with the other three items. The flavonoids found in cocoa are thought to benefit the heart in a couple of ways, including possible antioxidant protection.

You'll find a variety of chocolate recipes in Chapter 8 to soothe your cravings, including:

- One-Bowl Brownies
- Triple-Chocolate Decadence Cookies
- Earthquake Cake
- Texas Sheet Cake
- Fudge-Truffle Cheesecake
- Easy Cocoa Ice Cream
- Chocolate Lava Brownies

Every Little Bit Helps

Whether we're talking about light recipes for brownies or macaroni and cheese, the calorie and fat savings can really add up over time. If you have one serving of each of the top three comfort foods each week, by choosing the lighter version you save 296 calories and 37.3 grams of fat. This means you would shave off 1,184 calories and 148 grams of fat each month, or 15,392 calories and 1,940 grams of fat each year—just by switching to the lighter comfort foods once a week! Even if you aren't worried about excess calories, these comfort food recipes are lower in fat, saturated fat, cholesterol, and sometimes sugar and sodium, too. Whenever possible, we also give the recipes a fiber boost. These are all good practices to follow whether you're interested in reducing your risk of heart disease, cancer, or diabetes or whether you're lactose intolerant or suffer from acid reflux.

I hope you enjoy cooking with this cookbook as much as I enjoyed writing it. For four wonderful months, I tackled as many of the top comfort foods as was humanly possible—cutting extra calories from fat and sugar as I went along. Never have I felt more comforted while finishing a cookbook! Life is too short not to enjoy the foods we love—we can have our comfort foods and eat light, too. It just takes a little motivation and a really good cookbook. I hope you think you've found it.

CHAPTER TWO

Comforting the Carnivores

For many folks, meat–laden entrées are at the top of their personal comfort foods list. This chapter tackles most of the specific meaty dishes that people named in the allrecipes.com comfort food survey, proving that you can have your meat and eat light, too.

All-American Meatloaf

Makes 6 servings

I love that this meatloaf is so moist and loaded with vegetables. The original recipe called for two high-fat meats: ground pork and ground beef. For the light version, I ground up one of the leanest pork cuts, the tenderloin. I also used a ground sirloin and egg substitute to keep it lean and light.

3 slices whole-wheat or fiber-enriched white bread

1 large carrot, cut into ¼-inch-thick [6-mm] slices

1 large rib celery, coarsely chopped

½ cup [80 g] chopped onion

2 teaspoons [6 g] minced or chopped garlic

½ cup [90 g] fresh flat-leaf parsley, loosely packed (regular parsley can be used)

¾ pound [340 g] superlean ground beef or ground sirloin

¾ pound [340 g] ground pork tenderloin (ask your butcher to grind a pork tenderloin for you, or do it yourself using a food processor)

½ cup plus 3 tablespoons [165 g] ketchup, divided

4 teaspoons [18 g] mustard powder, divided

½ cup [130 g] egg substitute

1 teaspoon [6 g] salt

1 teaspoon [6 g] freshly ground black pepper

1 teaspoon [6 g] Tabasco sauce

1 teaspoon [1 g] chopped fresh rosemary, plus a teaspoon [1 g] for sprinkling

2 tablespoons [18 g] brown sugar

1. Preheat the oven to 400°F [200°C]. Remove the crusts from the bread and place the slices in the bowl of your food processor. Process until fine crumbs form (about 5 to 10 seconds). Add the bread crumbs to the bowl of an electric mixer.

2. Place the carrot, celery, onion, garlic, and parsley in the food processor and process until the vegetables are finely minced (about 30 seconds). Add the vegetables to the bowl with the bread crumbs.

3. Then add the ground beef and pork, ½ cup [120 g] of the ketchup, 2 teaspoons [9 g] of the mustard, the egg substitute, salt, pepper, Tabasco, and 1 teaspoon [1 g] of the rosemary to the mixing bowl and beat on low speed to blend well. Spoon the mixture into a 2-quart [2 l] casserole dish and press firmly into the shape of the dish.

4. Add the remaining 3 tablespoons [45 g] of ketchup, 2 teaspoons [9 g] of mustard, and brown sugar to a small bowl and mix until smooth. Spoon this mixture over the meatloaf.

5. Bake for 30 minutes. Sprinkle the remaining teaspoon of rosemary on top. Bake for another 30 minutes, or until cooked throughout. Let the meatloaf cool for 15 minutes before cutting it into slices.

Nutritional Analyses (per serving)

	BEFORE	AFTER		BEFORE	AFTER
Calories	341	227	Cholesterol	146 mg	68 mg
Protein	25 g	27 g	Fiber	1.8 g	2.1 g
Carbohydrates	18 g	18 g	Sodium	886 mg	883 mg
Fat	19 g	5.5 g	% Calories from Fat	50	22
Saturated Fat	7 g	1.9 g	Omega-3 Fatty Acids	.1 g	.1 g
Monounsaturated Fat	8 g	2.1 g	Omega-6 Fatty Acids	1.5 g	.3 g
Polyunsaturated Fat	1.6 g	.6 g			

Glazed Meatloaf

Makes 8 servings

If you like your meatloaf with a touch of sweetness, this is your ticket to a satisfying meal.

Canola oil cooking spray
½ cup [120 g] ketchup
¼ cup [1 g] packed dark brown sugar
¼ cup [61 g] lemon juice, divided
1 teaspoon [6 g] mustard powder
2 pounds [907 g] superlean ground beef or
    ground sirloin

4 slices whole-grain bread or higher-fiber
    white bread, broken up into small pieces
    (about 2 cups [70 g] of soft cubes)
⅔ cup [72 g] finely chopped onion
¼ cup [63 g] egg substitute
1 teaspoon [6 g] low-sodium beef-broth
    powder or granules

1. Preheat the oven to 350°F [180°C]. Coat a 9 x 5-inch [23 x 13-cm] loaf pan with the cooking spray.

2. In a small bowl, combine the ketchup, brown sugar, 1 tablespoon [15 g] of the lemon juice, and the mustard; set aside.

3. In the bowl of an electric mixer, combine the ground beef, bread pieces, onion, egg substitute, beef-broth powder, remaining 3 tablespoons [46 g] of lemon juice, and one-third of the ketchup mixture and beat on low speed until blended. Press the mixture into the prepared loaf pan.

4. Bake for 1 hour. Coat the top with the remaining ketchup mixture and bake for 10 additional minutes.

Nutritional Analyses (per serving)

	BEFORE	AFTER		BEFORE	AFTER
Calories	328	218	Cholesterol	101 mg	60 mg
Protein	23 g	24 g	Fiber	1 g	1.2 g
Carbohydrates	20 g	19.5 g	Sodium	430 mg	417 mg
Fat	17 g	5.4 g	% Calories from Fat	47	22
Saturated Fat	6.5 g	2 g	Omega-3 Fatty Acids	.1 g	.1 g
Monounsaturated Fat	7 g	2 g	Omega-6 Fatty Acids	.8 g	.1 g
Polyunsaturated Fat	1 g	.5 g			

Rock Salt-Roasted Chicken

Makes about 4 servings

This is a traditional Argentinean dish made when there isn't much time to cook dinner. With this recipe, you put it together quickly and then leave it in the oven to cook for an hour.

2½ pounds [1.2 kg] rock salt
1 whole roasting chicken, giblets removed
1 extra-large lemon, quartered

Salt
Freshly ground black pepper

1. Preheat the oven to 350°F [180°C]. Line a 9 x 13-inch [23 x 33-cm] baking pan with aluminum foil. Pour the rock salt evenly into the bottom of the pan.

2. Place the whole chicken, breast side up, on top of the rock salt. Remove as many seeds as you can from the quartered lemon. Lift the skin away from the breast and thigh areas and squeeze the lemon between the meat and the skin. Sprinkle a few pinches of salt and freshly ground pepper between the skin and meat as well.

3. Place the baking pan in the oven and bake the chicken, uncovered, for exactly 1 hour. Insert a fork into the thickest part of the chicken to make sure it's cooked throughout.

4. Remove the baking pan from the oven and let the chicken cool for 10 minutes. To eat, just pull off the part of the chicken desired—drumstick, thigh, breast, wing, etc.—and peel off the skin (and discard), leaving moist and tasty chicken meat.

Nutritional Analyses (per serving)

	BEFORE	AFTER		BEFORE	AFTER
Calories	282	223	Cholesterol	112 mg	106 mg
Protein	35.5 g	34 g	Fiber	.1 g	.1 g
Carbohydrates	1.5 g	1.5 g	Sodium	98 mg	95 mg
Fat	14.1 g	8.2 g	% Calories from Fat	45	33
Saturated Fat	4 g	2.3 g	Omega-3 Fatty Acids	.2 g	.1 g
Monounsaturated Fat	5.5 g	3 g	Omega-6 Fatty Acids	2.8 g	1.6 g
Polyunsaturated Fat	3.1 g	1.8 g			

Chicken Saté Skewers

Makes 5 servings (about 4 skewers each)

You can grill or barbecue these chicken skewers instead of broiling them—either way works great.

4 skinless, boneless chicken breasts

¼ cup [64 g] lower-sodium soy sauce

⅛ cup [42 g] dark molasses

⅛ cup [28 g] packed brown sugar

2 teaspoons [6 g] minced or chopped garlic

½ tablespoon [7 g] no or low-trans margarine

Juice of ½ large lemon

1. Soak 20 bamboo skewers in water. Cover one chicken breast with wax paper and pound it with a meat mallet until it's ¼ inch [6 mm] thick. Repeat with the other breasts. Cut each into five long strips.

2. In a small saucepan, combine the soy sauce, molasses, brown sugar, and garlic over medium heat and stir until the sugar dissolves (about 1 to 2 minutes). Turn off the heat.

3. Add the margarine and lemon juice and continue stirring until the margarine has melted.

4. Place the chicken in a dish and pour the sauce over the top. Cover and refrigerate for 6 to 8 hours.

5. Thread each strip of chicken onto one of the bamboo skewers and broil on a foil-lined cookie sheet, about 6 inches [15 cm] from the flame, until the top is nicely browned (about 2 minutes). Flip the skewers over and brown the other side (about 2 minutes). Serve!

Nutritional Analyses (per serving—the "after" figures include half of the marinade.)

	BEFORE	AFTER		BEFORE	AFTER
Calories	236	155	Cholesterol	84 mg	58 mg
Protein	17 g	22 g	Fiber	0 g	0 g
Carbohydrates	6 g	10 g	Sodium	974 mg	264 mg
Fat	16 g	2.8 g	% Calories from Fat	62	16
Saturated Fat	8 g	.3 g	Omega-3 Fatty Acids	0 g	.4 g
Monounsaturated Fat	5.5 g	1.3 g	Omega-6 Fatty Acids	2 g	6 g
Polyunsaturated Fat	2 g	1 g			

Oven-Fried Buttermilk Chicken

Makes 4 servings

To make this chicken crispy, coat it with canola oil cooking spray and then bake it in the oven followed by a quick turn under the broiler. This chicken is great served cold, too!

1 whole chicken, cut into pieces
1 cup [245 g] low-fat buttermilk
1 cup [125 g] unbleached white flour
1 teaspoon [6 g] salt
½ teaspoon [3 g] white pepper

½ teaspoon [3 g] ground chipotle pepper, or to taste (cayenne pepper can be substituted)
¼ teaspoon [1.5 g] ground cumin
Canola oil cooking spray

1. Remove the skin from the chicken pieces and discard. Put the chicken and buttermilk in a gallon-size [4 l] zip-top bag or a medium-sized bowl and refrigerate for several hours.

2. Preheat the oven to 450°F [230°C]. Add the flour, salt, white pepper, chipotle pepper, and cumin to a new gallon-size [4 l] zip-top bag. Stir with a fork to blend well.

3. Remove a piece of chicken from the buttermilk and shake off the excess. Dip the chicken into the flour mixture to coat. Holding the chicken over a plate, spray it well with the cooking spray. Dip the chicken into the flour mixture again and spray with the cooking spray. Place the chicken, bone side down, on a cookie sheet. Repeat with the remaining pieces of chicken.

4. Bake the chicken until it is cooked throughout and the coating is golden brown (about 25 to 30 minutes). Switch the oven to "broil" and cook the chicken 6 inches [15 cm] from the heat for a minute or two (until the outside is browned); watch it so it doesn't burn.

Nutritional Analyses (per serving of light or dark meat)

	BEFORE	AFTER		BEFORE	AFTER
Calories	473	283	Cholesterol	160 mg	122 mg
Protein	34 g	41 g	Fiber	1 g	.2 g
Carbohydrates	18 g	6 g	Sodium	886 mg	275 mg
Fat	29 g	9 g	% Calories from Fat	55	29
Saturated Fat	8 g	2.6 g	Omega-3 Fatty Acids	.4 g	.2 g
Monounsaturated Fat	12 g	3.4 g	Omega-6 Fatty Acids	6.3 g	1.8 g
Polyunsaturated Fat	7 g	2.1 g			

Turkey Burgers

Makes 4 servings

This flavorful ground-turkey burger is a smart alternative to the more common ground-beef burger. Don't worry about adding cheese to this burger; it tastes delicious on its own. The burgers go great with whole-grain hamburger buns, plus some sliced tomato and lettuce leaves.

1 pound [454 g] extra-lean (99% fat-free) or lean (93% fat-free) ground turkey

¼ cup [27 g] fine, dry plain bread crumbs

¼ cup [63 g] egg substitute (1 large egg, beaten, can be substituted)

2 tablespoons [12 g] finely minced (white and part of green) green onion

2 tablespoons [36 g] lower-sodium soy sauce

1 teaspoon [3 g] minced or chopped garlic

1 teaspoon [3g] minced fresh or bottled ginger

Canola oil cooking spray

1. Combine the ground turkey, bread crumbs, egg substitute, green onion, soy sauce, garlic, and ginger in a large bowl and blend together well by hand or on the low speed of an electric mixer. Shape into 4 patties.

2. Coat a large nonstick skillet with the cooking spray and heat over medium heat. Add the burgers to the skillet and cook until cooked throughout (about 5 minutes on each side).

3. Serve with a slice of tomato, crispy lettuce leaves, and any lower-calorie condiments you might desire (ketchup or mustard).

Nutritional Analyses (The "before" figures are per serving, not including the bun. The "after" figures are per serving, using 93% fat-free ground turkey and not including the bun.)

	BEFORE	AFTER		BEFORE	AFTER
Calories	283	190	Cholesterol	127 mg	90 mg
Protein	24 g	22 g	Fiber	.3 g	.2 g
Carbohydrates	6 g	2.5 g	Sodium	583 mg	441 mg
Fat	17 g	9.5 g	% Calories from Fat	54	45
Saturated Fat	7 g	2.5 g	Omega-3 Fatty Acids	.1 g	.1 g
Monounsaturated Fat	7.4 g	3.5 g	Omega-6 Fatty Acids	.7 g	2.1 g
Polyunsaturated Fat	.8 g	2.3 g			

Homemade Sloppy Joes

Makes 4 sandwiches

Sloppy Joes are a quick meal that will appeal to everyone at your dinner table. I don't suggest using those prepackaged Sloppy Joe mixes, so try this easy-to-make homemade version. The Joes will be getting sloppy in about 20 minutes.

1 pound [454 g] superlean ground beef or
   ground sirloin
½ cup [80 g] chopped onion
½ cup [75 g] chopped green bell pepper
¾ cup plus 2 tablespoons [210 g] ketchup
½ cup [119 g] water
2 tablespoons [28 g] packed brown sugar
1 tablespoon [16 g] prepared mustard
½ teaspoon [1 g] garlic powder

½ teaspoon [3 g] salt (optional)
½ teaspoon [3 g] black pepper
   (add more to taste)
4 multigrain or whole-wheat hamburger buns
   or rolls
1 to 2 ounces [29 to 57 g] shredded
   reduced-fat Monterey Jack or Cheddar
   cheese (optional)

1. Brown the ground beef, onion, and green pepper over medium heat in a large nonstick skillet.

2. Stir in the ketchup, water, brown sugar, mustard, and garlic powder; mix thoroughly. Reduce the heat to simmer, cover, and let simmer for 20 minutes, stirring every 5 minutes or so.

3. Add salt (if desired) and pepper to taste and stir. Serve one-fourth of the mixture over the bottom of a split multigrain bun or roll. Sprinkle each with a tablespoon or two of cheese, if desired. Serve with or without the top of the bun or roll.

Nutritional Analyses (per serving)

	BEFORE	AFTER		BEFORE	AFTER
Calories	511	389	Cholesterol	89 mg	70 mg
Protein	30 g	31 g	Fiber	3 g	5 g
Carbohydrates	47 g	48 g	Sodium	1,066 mg	1,062 mg
Fat	23 g	10 g	% Calories from Fat	41	23
Saturated Fat	10 g	4.4 g	Omega-3 Fatty Acids	.1 g	.1 g
Monounsaturated Fat	8.6 g	2.5 g	Omega-6 Fatty Acids	1.7 g	.9 g
Polyunsaturated Fat	1.9 g	1.5 g			

Spicy Fried Chicken

Makes 4 servings

Cold spicy fried chicken brings visions of summer picnics dancing in my head. Since I'm a bit of a hot-spice wimp, I made a kid-friendly version for me (and the kids) and you spice lovers out there will just have to add more Cajun spice per your personal "heat" threshold. The biggest change I made to give this recipe a healthful boost is to pan-fry the chicken in a little bit of canola oil to brown the coating, then finish by baking it in the oven, instead of deep-frying.

Canola oil cooking spray

4 skinless chicken breasts

½ cup [62 g] unbleached white flour

½ cup [24 g] mashed potato flakes

1½ to 3 teaspoons [3 to 6 g] Creole or Cajun seasoning, to taste

¾ teaspoon [4 g] salt

1 teaspoon [2 g] ground oregano

½ teaspoon [3 g] black pepper

½ teaspoon [3 g] garlic powder

1 egg

¾ cup [185 g] low-fat or whole milk

1½ tablespoons [20 g] canola oil

1. Preheat the oven to 450°F [230°C]. Line a 9 x 9-inch [23 x 23-cm] baking dish with aluminum foil and coat the foil-covered dish with the cooking spray.

2. Rinse the chicken breasts and pat them dry with paper towels; set aside.

3. Place the flour, potato flakes, Creole seasoning, salt, oregano, pepper, and garlic powder in a small bowl; stir to blend well.

4. Add the egg and milk to a separate small bowl and beat with a fork until smooth.

5. Warm a large, heavy skillet over medium-high heat. Add the oil, spreading it evenly over the bottom of the skillet, and let the oil get hot.

6. Dip each chicken breast first in the flour mixture, then in the egg mixture, and then back in the flour mixture. Place the chicken in the hot skillet. Repeat with the remaining chicken breasts. Spray the tops of the chicken with the cooking spray.

7. When the bottom of each breast is nicely browned, turn it over with a spatula and brown the other side. When both sides have browned, remove each chicken breast and place it in the prepared baking dish.

8. Finish cooking the chicken breasts by baking them in the oven for about 15 minutes (or until the thickest part of the breast is cooked throughout).

Nutritional Analyses (per serving)

	BEFORE	AFTER		BEFORE	AFTER
Calories	410	223	Cholesterol	107 mg	82 mg
Protein	32 g	29 g	Fiber	.4 g	.4 g
Carbohydrates	9 g	8.5 g	Sodium	299 mg	284 mg
Fat	27 g	7 g	% Calories from Fat	59	28
Saturated Fat	8 g	1 g	Omega-3 Fatty Acids	.6 g	.5 g
Monounsaturated Fat	10 g	3.6 g	Omega-6 Fatty Acids	7 g	1.4 g
Polyunsaturated Fat	8 g	1.9 g			

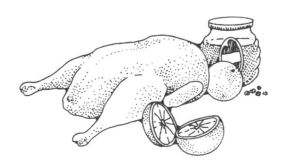

Prosciutto Chicken

Makes 4 servings

Make moist, oven-fried chicken breasts topped with prosciutto slices, condensed chicken broth, and grated Fontina cheese. It sounds simple, but it tastes heavenly! I lightened the original recipe, which used twice the cheese, butter, and chicken with the skin.

4 skinless, boneless chicken breasts
1 cup [125 g] unbleached white flour
1 teaspoon [2 g] freshly ground black pepper
1 teaspoon [6 g] salt
¼ teaspoon [.65 g] cayenne pepper
2 teaspoons [10 g] canola oil

Canola oil cooking spray
¼ cup [60 g] double-strength or condensed low-sodium chicken broth
1½ ounces [41 g] prosciutto (about 4 thin slices)
2 ounces [57 g] grated Fontina cheese

1. Preheat the oven to 400°F [200°C]. Line a 9 x 13-inch [23 x 33-cm] baking dish with aluminum foil. Wash the chicken pieces and dry well with paper towels.

2. Place the flour, black pepper, salt, and cayenne pepper in a gallon-size zip-top freezer bag and shake vigorously to blend. Add the chicken, one piece at a time, to the bag filled with the seasoned flour. Shake the bag again to coat the chicken well.

3. Add the oil to a large nonstick skillet, spreading it out to cover the bottom of the skillet. Place the skillet on medium heat. When the oil is hot, add the chicken pieces to the skillet, lightly coat the tops with the cooking spray, and brown the chicken on both sides.

4. Place the chicken in the prepared baking dish, drizzle each chicken breast with 1½ teaspoons [8 g] of chicken broth, then cover each with a prosciutto slice and sprinkle the Fontina evenly over the tops. Drizzle the remaining chicken broth evenly over the grated cheese.

5. Bake the chicken in the center of the oven for about 25 minutes, or until the breasts are cooked throughout and the cheese is bubbly. Serve with steamed rice and vegetables.

Nutritional Analyses (per serving)

	BEFORE	AFTER		BEFORE	AFTER
Calories	402	267	Cholesterol	134 mg	93 mg
Protein	40 g	34 g	Fiber	.3 g	.3 g
Carbohydrates	8 g	7 g	Sodium	674 mg	496 mg
Fat	23 g	10 g	% Calories from Fat	51	34
Saturated Fat	11 g	4 g	Omega-3 Fatty Acids	.4 g	.4 g
Monounsaturated Fat	7.5 g	4 g	Omega-6 Fatty Acids	1.9 g	1.2 g
Polyunsaturated Fat	2.5 g	1.6 g			

Marinated Flank Steak

Makes 6 servings (about 3 ounces [85 g] cooked per serving
if using a 1½-pound [680-g] flank)

There's just something about marinated flank steak that looks, smells, and tastes spectacular. The steak tastes wonderful all by itself, but the slices can also be cut into bite-size pieces and tossed into a cold pasta salad. I cut the sodium by using lower-sodium soy sauce and dropping the garlic salt and opting for some garlic powder instead. I substituted some concentrated chicken broth instead of a lot of oil, but I used a low-sodium brand. I also added less oil in the marinade to cut down on the added fat and calories in the meat.

6 tablespoons [90 g] concentrated chicken broth (lower-sodium if available)

½ cup [170 g] honey

½ cup [128 g] lower-sodium soy sauce

2 tablespoons [28 g] canola oil

4 green onions (white and part of green), cut into thin, diagonal slices

2 teaspoons [11 g] Worcestershire sauce

1 teaspoon [2 g] ground ginger
    (or 2 teaspoons [4 g] minced fresh ginger)

1 teaspoon [6 g] garlic powder
    (or 2 teaspoons [5 g] minced fresh garlic)

1 medium-large flank steak
    (about 1½ pounds [680 g] at least)

1. In a medium bowl, whisk together the chicken broth, honey, soy sauce, oil, green onions, Worcestershire sauce, ginger, and garlic powder; set aside.

2. Remove any visible fat from the flank steak. Lightly score the meat with a serrated knife, about ¼ inch [6 mm] into the meat, in a crisscross pattern (about an inch between cuts) on the top and bottom of the steak.

3. Place the steak in a rectangular plastic container, add the marinade, and coat the steak well. Cover and marinate the flank steak all day or overnight, flipping it occasionally.

4. Grill the steak about 10 to 15 minutes on each side, or until cooked to the desired doneness. Using a carving knife, cut diagonally across the grain of the meat into slices of desired thickness.

Nutritional Analyses (per serving)

	BEFORE	AFTER		BEFORE	AFTER
Calories	337	232	Cholesterol	59 mg	57 mg
Protein	23 g	24 g	Fiber	.2 g	.2 g
Carbohydrates	13 g	13 g	Sodium	968 mg	488 mg
Fat	21 g	9 g	% Calories from Fat	56	35
Saturated Fat	6.3 g	3.8 g	Omega-3 Fatty Acids	.2 g	.1 g
Monounsaturated Fat	7.2 g	3.7 g	Omega-6 Fatty Acids	5.6 g	.3 g
Polyunsaturated Fat	5.8 g	.5 g			

Savory Pot Roast with Veggies

Makes about 8 servings

I've got to admit that good old pot roast is a well-balanced meal, made all in one pot. The key is to take a very lean cut of beef and cook it over low heat for several hours (to tenderize) and create tasty juices. It's easy to throw some veggies into the mix, too, which is always a good thing to do. There are all sorts of pot roast recipes and variations, but I thought I would lighten up one that's easy and basic. You can add your own ingredient twists and tastes if you desire.

¼ cup [31 g] unbleached white flour

½ teaspoon [3 g] salt

¼ teaspoon [1 g] black pepper

3½ pounds [1,587 g] rump roast (trimmed of visible fat)

1 tablespoon [14 g] canola oil

2 medium onions, cut in half and sliced

3 medium to large potatoes, quartered

1 (14½-ounce [411-g]) can petite diced tomatoes (low-sodium if available)

2 cups [256 g] baby carrots, cut in half

1 cup [244 g] low-sodium beef broth

2 tablespoons [7 g] minced fresh parsley

½ teaspoon [3 g] garlic powder

1 cup [242 g] fat-free sour cream (optional)

1. Combine the flour, salt, and pepper in a medium-sized shallow bowl and stir with a fork or whisk. Coat all sides of the rump roast with the mixture, pressing it firmly into each side.

2. Add the oil to a large nonstick saucepan and heat over medium-high heat. Add the roast to the hot oil and brown on all sides. Reduce the heat to low and add the onions. Cook for about 5 minutes, stirring occasionally. Add the potatoes, tomatoes, carrots, beef broth, parsley, and garlic powder; stir well. Cover the saucepan tightly with the lid and reduce the heat to simmer. Simmer for about 4 hours, turning the roast and gently stirring the vegetables occasionally.

3. Remove the roast from the saucepan and let it sit for 10 minutes. Remove the vegetables with a slotted spoon and place them in a serving bowl. Stir the sour cream into the juice remaining in the saucepan, if desired. If you don't want to add the sour cream, you can slice the pot roast and serve the slices with the vegetables and the pan juices.

Nutritional Analyses (per serving)

	BEFORE	AFTER		BEFORE	AFTER
Calories	477	380	Cholesterol	85 mg	82 mg
Protein	32.5 g	34 g	Fiber	4.6 g	4.6 g
Carbohydrates	34 g	34 g	Sodium	440 mg	444 mg
Fat	23 g	11 g	% Calories from Fat	43	26
Saturated Fat	7 g	3.7 g	Omega-3 Fatty Acids	.2 g	.2 g
Monounsaturated Fat	8.8 g	4.9 g	Omega-6 Fatty Acids	4.5 g	.8 g
Polyunsaturated Fat	4.8 g	1 g			

Herb-Roasted Turkey Breast with Apple Cider Gravy

Makes 4 to 6 servings

My family loves Thanksgiving dinner, and this recipe is a way to make just enough turkey so that your family can enjoy it at any time of the year. I chose to roast a turkey breast not only because it's lower in fat than dark turkey meat but also because it's the perfect size for a family of four. Using a couple of recipes as my guide, I basically cut out the butter used to roast the turkey and make the gravy. I also skinned the turkey breast, because that's an easy way to cut the fat in half right off the bat. To keep the meat moist and flavorful, though, I rubbed it with a little canola oil, then added an herb rub. The browned bits at the bottom of the roasting pan and any turkey broth left after roasting are used to make a flavorful gravy, with the addition of apple cider and fat-free half-and-half.

1 turkey breast (about 2 to 3 pounds [907 to 1,361 g]), skin removed
1½ teaspoons [7 g] canola oil

DRY RUB
2 teaspoons [3 g] finely chopped fresh flat-leaf parsley
2 teaspoons [2 g] finely chopped fresh thyme
2 teaspoons [2 g] finely chopped fresh marjoram
2 teaspoons [2 g] finely chopped fresh sage
¼ teaspoon [1 g] salt
¼ teaspoon [1 g] black pepper

GRAVY
¼ cup [60 g] turkey broth (from the pan drippings), plus extra chicken broth if not enough turkey drippings to equal ¼ cup [60 g]
Canola oil cooking spray
¼ cup [40 g] finely chopped onion
¼ teaspoon [.5 g] finely chopped fresh sage (ground sage can be substituted)
¼ cup [62 g] apple cider
2 teaspoons [5 g] all-purpose flour
2 tablespoons [30 g] fat-free half-and-half
Salt and black pepper to taste

1. Preheat the oven to 425°F [220°C]. Rub the outside of the turkey breast with the oil. Combine the rub ingredients in a small bowl and toss to blend well. Rub the outside of the turkey with the mixture.

2. Place the turkey breast in a small roasting pan or similar pan (with or without a rack in the bottom) and roast, covered, for 30 minutes.

3. Reduce the oven temperature to 350°F [180°C], and baste the turkey with any pan drippings. Continue to roast, uncovered, for 30 minutes or until the thickest part of the breast is cooked throughout.

4. Transfer the turkey to a serving platter and let it cool for 15 minutes. While you are waiting, pour the turkey drippings and any browned bits from the bottom of the roasting pan into a measuring cup (hopefully, you will have about ¼ cup [60 g]—if not, you can add some chicken broth to equal that amount).

5. For the gravy, start heating a small nonstick saucepan over medium-high heat. When the pan is hot, coat it with the cooking spray and add the chopped onion. Lightly brown the onion, stirring occasionally (about 3 minutes). Add the sage and cook, stirring, for 30 to 60 seconds. Reduce the heat to simmer, and stir in the reserved turkey drippings and the apple cider. In a small cup, blend the flour with the half-and-half and quickly whisk the mixture into the saucepan with the gravy. Continue to simmer for about 2 to 4 minutes, whisking occasionally, until nicely thickened. Season with salt and pepper if to taste. Carve the turkey into slices and serve topped with your homemade gravy.

Nutritional Analyses (per serving of turkey)

	BEFORE	AFTER		BEFORE	AFTER
Calories	347	254	Cholesterol	204 mg	149 mg
Protein	66 g	54 g	Fiber	0 g	0 g
Carbohydrates	0 g	0 g	Sodium	120 mg	210 mg
Fat	7.3 g	2.7 g	% Calories from Fat	19	10
Saturated Fat	2 g	.5 g	Omega-3 Fatty Acids	.1 g	.2 g
Monounsaturated Fat	2.7 g	1.1 g	Omega-6 Fatty Acids	1.5 g	.6 g
Polyunsaturated Fat	1.7 g	.8 g			

Nutritional Analyses (per serving of cider gravy)

	BEFORE	AFTER		BEFORE	AFTER
Calories	128	24	Cholesterol	19 mg	.4 mg
Protein	.4 g	1.3 g	Fiber	.3 g	.3 g
Carbohydrates	4 g	4.4 g	Sodium	4 mg	88 mg
Fat	12.5 g	.2 g	% Calories from Fat	88	75
Saturated Fat	4.4 g	.05 g	Omega-3 Fatty Acids	.2 g	0 g
Monounsaturated Fat	5 g	.1 g	Omega-6 Fatty Acids	2.3 g	.03 g
Polyunsaturated Fat	2.5 g	.04 g			

CHAPTER THREE

Pasta, Pies, and Casseroles to Warm Your Soul

What says "comfort" better than those beloved pasta dishes and casseroles so many of us grew up with? No favorite pasta or casserole recipe is left uncovered in this chapter. From tuna casserole to chicken pot pie, macaroni and cheese to spaghetti with meatballs, light recipes for all tastes are right at your fingertips.

Beef Sheperd's Pie

Makes 6 servings

Sheperd's pie is so comforting. This version features lean sirloin tip roast or ground sirloin and a quick gravy made from beef broth or consommé, ketchup, and fat-free half-and-half. Also, this is a great recipe if you have some leftover roast beef or lean steak. If you decide to use ground sirloin, follow the cooking instructions in the note following the recipe.

4 large potatoes, peeled and cubed

¼ cup [28 g] shredded reduced-fat sharp Cheddar cheese

1 tablespoon [14 g] butter or no-trans margarine

1 tablespoon [10 g] minced onion

Salt and black pepper to taste

Canola oil cooking spray

1 teaspoon [5 g] canola oil

1 cup [128 g] diced carrots

½ cup [80 g] chopped onion

1½ teaspoons [4 g] minced or chopped garlic

1½ tablespoons [12 g] all-purpose flour

¼ cup [61 g] fat-free half-and-half

¾ cup [183 g] low-sodium beef broth or canned consommé

2 tablespoons [30 g] ketchup

2 cups [280 g] (grilled or cooked) sirloin tip roast, chopped and trimmed of visible fat (or 14 ounces [397 g] ground sirloin or ground superlean beef, browned*)

½ cup [72 g] frozen petite peas

Paprika (optional)

1. Bring a large saucepan of water to a boil. Add the potatoes and cook until tender but firm (about 15 minutes). Drain the potatoes well, place them in the bowl of an electric mixer, and mash by beating on low speed. Add the Cheddar, butter, and onion. Add salt and pepper to taste.

2. Preheat the oven to 375°F [190°C]. Coat a 2-quart [2 l] casserole dish with the cooking spray.

3. Add the oil to large nonstick skillet and heat over medium-high heat. Add the carrots, onion, and garlic and cook for 3 to 4 minutes. Meanwhile, add the flour to a small cup and slowly stir in the half-and-half to make a thin paste.

4. Add the beef broth, ketchup, and half-and-half mixture to the skillet. Then put the cooked beef in the skillet and stir. Bring to a boil, reduce the heat, and simmer for about 3 to 4 minutes (or until nicely thickened). Stir in the peas.

5. Spread the beef and vegetable mixture in the bottom of the prepared casserole dish. Top with the mashed potato mixture. Spray the top with cooking spray, and sprinkle with paprika, if desired.

6. Bake for 20 minutes, or until the mashed potatoes are golden brown.

*Note If you're using ground beef for the recipe, brown the beef in a large nonstick skillet coated with cooking spray. Use a potato masher to mash the beef while it's cooking to create smaller browned pieces.

Nutritional Analyses (per serving)

	BEFORE	AFTER		BEFORE	AFTER
Calories	460	377	Cholesterol	82 mg	42 mg
Protein	20 g	22 g	Fiber	4.5 g	7 g
Carbohydrates	42 g	60 g	Sodium	948 mg	149 mg
Fat	24 g	6 g	% Calories from Fat	45	14
Saturated Fat	12 g	2 g	Omega-3 Fatty Acids	0 g	.2 g
Monounsaturated Fat	8 g	1.9 g	Omega-6 Fatty Acids	3 g	.5 g
Polyunsaturated Fat	3 g	1 g			

Chile Rellenos Casserole

Makes 6 entrée servings

I love chiles rellenos and this is a great way to get the taste of rellenos but without a lot of the prep work. Using half eggs and half egg substitute, reduced-fat cheese, superlean ground beef, fat-free half-and-half, and low-fat milk takes this comfort food from bad to good. It takes 10 minutes to throw together and then 55 minutes to bake.

Canola oil cooking spray

1 pound [454 g] superlean ground beef or ground sirloin

1 cup [160 g] chopped onions

3 large eggs

⅔ cup [188 g] egg substitute

½ cup [63 g] Wondra quick-mixing flour

1 cup [247 g] low-fat milk

1 cup [242 g] fat-free half-and-half

½ teaspoon [3 g] salt

½ teaspoon [3 g] black pepper

3 (7-ounce [199-g]) cans whole green chile peppers, drained, then sliced open

2 cups [226 g] shredded reduced-fat Monterey Jack and sharp Cheddar cheese, divided

1. Preheat the oven to 350°F [180°C]. Coat a 9 x 13-inch [23 x 33-cm] baking dish with the cooking spray.

2. In a large nonstick skillet over medium-high heat, brown the beef and onions (about 6 to 10 minutes).

3. While you are waiting for the beef to brown, add the eggs, egg substitute, and flour to the bowl of an electric mixer and beat on medium speed to combine well. Add the milk, half-and-half, salt, and pepper to the egg mixture and beat on medium to combine (about 2 minutes).

4. Arrange half of the chile peppers, in a single layer, on the bottom of the prepared baking dish. Sprinkle half of the cheese and all of the meat mixture over the top.

5. Lay the remaining chile peppers over the meat in a single layer and pour the egg mixture over the peppers.

6. Bake, uncovered, for 45 minutes. Sprinkle the remaining cheese over the casserole and bake for 10 minutes longer. Let the casserole cool for about 5 minutes before cutting and serving.

Nutritional Analyses (per serving)

	BEFORE	AFTER		BEFORE	AFTER
Calories	461	293	Cholesterol	257 mg	129 mg
Protein	31 g	29 g	Fiber	4 g	4 g
Carbohydrates	21 g	21.5 g	Sodium	540 mg	530 mg
Fat	27 g	10 g	% Calories from Fat	53	31
Saturated Fat	14 g	5.7 g	Omega-3 Fatty Acids	.2 g	.2 g
Monounsaturated Fat	10 g	1.7 g	Omega-6 Fatty Acids	1 g	.6 g
Polyunsaturated Fat	1.5 g	1 g			

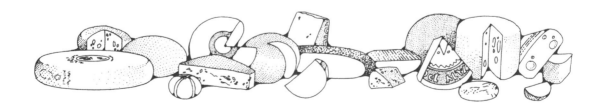

Cheddar-Crab Biscuit Pie

Makes 4 servings (2 slices each)

This savory dish makes a great dinner entrée or appetizer. It uses reduced-fat Bisquick baking mix along with reduced-fat Cheddar cheese and low-fat buttermilk. The only cooking fat added is a tablespoon of canola oil.

Canola oil cooking spray

2 cups [224 g] reduced-fat Bisquick
   baking mix

1½ cups [170 g] shredded reduced-fat sharp
   Cheddar cheese, divided

⅔ cup [184 g] low-fat buttermilk

1 tablespoon [14 g] canola oil

½ teaspoon [.2 g] dried parsley,
   finely crushed

¼ teaspoon [1 g] garlic powder

⅔ cup [101 g] fresh crabmeat in small pieces

1. Preheat the oven to 450°F [230°C]. Coat a 9-inch [23-cm] pie plate with the cooking spray.

2. Combine the Bisquick, 1 cup [113 g] of the Cheddar, the buttermilk, and oil in a medium-sized bowl. Stir with a wooden spoon, by hand, or with an electric mixer on low speed until well combined.

3. Pat the dough out into the prepared pie plate, creating a slight lip around the edge—like a pizza crust. Sprinkle the parsley and garlic powder over the top of the dough. Sprinkle the crabmeat evenly over the top of the dough. Sprinkle the remaining cheese over the crab.

4. Bake for 14 to 16 minutes, or until the cheese is nicely melted. Slice the pie like a pizza into 8 wedges and serve hot.

Nutritional Analyses (per serving)

	BEFORE	AFTER		BEFORE	AFTER
Calories	536	420	Cholesterol	82 mg	52 mg
Protein	20 g	22 g	Fiber	1 g	1 g
Carbohydrates	40 g	46 g	Sodium	1,176 mg	1,100 mg
Fat	33 g	15 g	% Calories from Fat	55	34
Saturated Fat	15.5 g	7.3 g	Omega-3 Fatty Acids	.7 g	.6 g
Monounsaturated Fat	11.5 g	2.2 g	Omega-6 Fatty Acids	1.1 g	1 g
Polyunsaturated Fat	2.6 g	2.2 g			

Contemporary Tuna Casserole

Makes 6 servings

This casserole doesn't use the standard cream of mushroom soup—you make your own sauce. Fresh vegetables add a nice crunch to the mix. The original recipe called for mayonnaise, but I used a lot less. I threw in some celery, too, and switched to reduced-fat Cheddar.

Canola oil cooking spray

6 cups [228 g] egg noodles or fettuccine (about 9 ounces [255 g] fresh), cooked

2 (6-ounce [170-g]) cans solid white tuna packed in water, drained and broken into small chunks

1 cup [120 g] chopped celery

½ cup [50 g] chopped green onions

½ cup [73 g] petite peas

1 cup [113 g] shredded reduced-fat sharp Cheddar cheese

½ cup plus 2 tablespoons [151 g] fat-free sour cream

¼ cup [58 g] light mayonnaise

2 teaspoons [10 g] prepared mustard

½ teaspoon [3 g] dried thyme

¼ teaspoon [1 g] salt

1 large tomato, chopped

1. Preheat the oven to 350°F [180°C]. Coat a 2-quart [2 l] casserole dish with the cooking spray.

2. In a large mixing bowl, toss together the cooked noodles, tuna, celery, green onions, and peas. Stir in half of the Cheddar, and the sour cream, mayonnaise, and mustard. Season with the thyme and salt.

3. Spoon the mixture into the prepared dish and sprinkle the top with the remaining Cheddar.

4. Bake for 30 minutes (until hot and bubbly). Sprinkle the tomatoes over the top before dishing it up.

Nutritional Analyses (per serving)

	BEFORE	AFTER		BEFORE	AFTER
Calories	621	396	Cholesterol	102 mg	83 mg
Protein	24 g	24 g	Fiber	3.3 g	4 g
Carbohydrates	45 g	50 g	Sodium	620 mg	548 mg
Fat	39 g	10 g	% Calories from Fat	57	23
Saturated Fat	9 g	4 g	Omega-3 Fatty Acids	2 g	.2 g
Monounsaturated Fat	11 g	1.6 g	Omega-6 Fatty Acids	11 g	1.3 g
Polyunsaturated Fat	17 g	1.7 g			

Spaghetti and Oven-Baked Meatballs

Makes 6 servings (2 meatballs each)

I tried making over quite a few high-profile meatball recipes, but this one ended up being my favorite. You roll the meatballs in bread crumbs, then spray with canola oil cooking spray and bake. The meatballs turn out to be crispy on the outside and moist on the inside.

SAUCE

1 tablespoon [14 g] canola oil
1 cup [160 g] finely chopped onions
1 cup [70 g] chopped crimini mushrooms
2 teaspoons [6 g] minced or chopped garlic
2 (15-ounce [425-g]) cans low-sodium tomato sauce
2 (6-ounce [170-g]) cans low-sodium tomato paste
1 (14½-ounce [411-g]) can petite vine-ripened tomatoes, diced and including liquid
1 tablespoon [13 g] sugar
2 teaspoons [4 g] dried oregano
¾ teaspoon [4 g] salt (optional)
½ teaspoon [3 g] freshly ground pepper
1 bay leaf

MEATBALLS

2 slices whole-wheat or fiber-enriched white bread
1 pound [454 g] extra-superlean or ground sirloin (9% fat or less)
1 large egg
¼ cup [63 g] egg substitute
⅓ cup [33 g] shredded or grated Parmesan cheese
2 to 3 tablespoons [8 to 11 g] finely chopped Italian parsley (regular parsley can be substituted)
1 teaspoon [3 g] minced or chopped garlic
1 teaspoon [2 g] dried oregano
½ teaspoon [3 g] salt (optional)
Dash or two of freshly ground black pepper
1 cup [108 g] Italian-style bread crumbs
Canola oil cooking spray
12 ounces [340 g] uncooked angel hair spaghetti

1. Preheat the oven to 400°F [200°C]. To make the sauce, heat the canola oil in a large non-stick saucepan over medium-high heat. Add the onions and mushrooms and sauté for about 5 minutes. Stir in the garlic and sauté for a minute longer.

2. Stir in the tomato sauce, tomato paste, diced tomatoes (with liquid), sugar, oregano, salt (if desired), pepper, and bay leaf. Reduce the heat to simmer, cover the saucepan, and cook for 30 minutes.

3. While the sauce is simmering, make the meatballs. Trim the crust off the bread slices and dice into small cubes with a serrated knife (you should have about 1 cup of bread cubes). Place the bread in a small bowl and drizzle with ¼ cup [59 ml] warm water; let soak for a few minutes. Using your hand, gently squeeze some of the excess water from the bread and place the bread in the bowl of an electric mixer. Add the ground beef, egg, egg substitute, Parmesan, parsley, garlic, oregano, salt (if desired), and pepper and beat on low just until well blended.

4. Using a ¼-cup [59-ml] measure, scoop the meat mixture to form each large meatball. Place the Italian-style bread crumbs in a shallow bowl. Coat each meatball in bread crumbs and place it on a cookie sheet coated with the cooking spray. Coat the tops and sides of the meatballs with the cooking spray. Bake for 40 minutes, or until the meatballs are cooked throughout and lightly browned on the outside. While the meatballs are baking, start boiling the spaghetti noodles according to the package instructions.

5. Add the meatballs to the spaghetti sauce and simmer for 30 minutes longer. Serve over hot spaghetti.

Nutritional Analyses (per serving)

	BEFORE	AFTER		BEFORE	AFTER
Calories	775	529	Cholesterol	123 mg	64 mg
Protein	34 g	29 g	Fiber	8 g	8 g
Carbohydrates	96 g	81 g	Sodium	1,319 mg	583 mg
Fat	29.5 g	10 g	% Calories from Fat	34	17
Saturated Fat	8 g	3 g	Omega-3 Fatty Acids	.2 g	.3 g
Monounsaturated Fat	9.4 g	4.5 g	Omega-6 Fatty Acids	9.4 g	1.3 g
Polyunsaturated Fat	9.6 g	2 g			

Chicken Pot Pie

Makes 6 servings

Many of the pot pies found in the frozen-food section of the grocery store contain more pastry and gravy than chicken and vegetables, which is why pot pie usually ends up being a calorie-heavy meal. I also understand that most people may not be enthusiastic about making a pie crust just to enjoy chicken pot pie. So you can cut the fat in a pot pie simply by eliminating the bottom crust and using a refrigerated prepared crust for the top crust. Trim the fat and calories further by using 1 teaspoon [5 g] of canola oil and canola oil cooking spray to sauté the vegetables, and instead of making the gravy with light whipping cream or half-and-half, use whole milk. The final result turns out rich-tasting and savory, with a golden, flaky top crust—just like a chicken pot pie should.

Canola oil cooking spray

1 teaspoon [5 g] canola oil

1 large onion, chopped

1 cup [70 g] sliced fresh mushrooms

¾ cup [113 g] sliced celery

½ cup [75 g] finely chopped red bell pepper

⅓ cup [42 g] all-purpose flour

1 teaspoon [6 g] poultry seasoning

¼ to ½ teaspoon [1 to 3 g] freshly ground black pepper

1 (14½-ounce [411-g] can) low-sodium chicken broth (or 1½ cups [360 g] broth made from packets or cubes)

1 cup [244 g] whole milk (2% low-fat milk or fat-free half-and-half can be substituted)

3 skinless chicken breasts, cooked and shredded into bite-size pieces*

1 cup [144 g] frozen peas

1 pie crust (packaged)

1. Preheat the oven to 400°F [200°C]. Spray a deep 9-inch [23-cm] cake pan with the cooking spray.

2. Add the oil to a large saucepan and let it warm. Add the onion, mushrooms, celery, and red pepper; spray the top of the vegetables with cooking spray. Cook for about 5 minutes, stirring frequently. Meanwhile, combine the flour, poultry seasoning, and black pepper in a small bowl and stir to blend.

3. Once the vegetables are just tender, stir in the flour mixture and immediately add the broth and milk all at once. Cook, stirring, over medium heat until thickened and bubbly (about 3 to 5 minutes). Turn off the heat and stir in the chicken and peas. Spoon the mixture into the prepared pan.

4. Lay the prepared crust over the chicken mixture. You will have extra pie crust around the edges of the pan, and you can handle this in three different ways. You can tuck the extra crust under to form a side crust, you can turn the edges of the crust under and flute the top edges of the dish, or you can trim the excess off with a knife and cut out small leaves or other shapes from these pieces and use them to decorate the top of the pie.

5. Place the cake pan on a large cookie sheet or jelly-roll pan (in case the pot pie bubbles over) and bake for about 30 minutes, or until the crust is golden brown. Cool for 15 minutes before serving.

*Note If you aren't using leftover chicken to make this recipe, add the chicken broth from the recipe and the raw chicken breasts to a medium-sized saucepan. Bring the broth to a boil, cover the pan, and reduce the heat to the lowest setting. Simmer until the chicken is cooked throughout (about 20 to 30 minutes). Remove the chicken and shred for the recipe; the chicken broth can still be used in the recipe, too.

Nutritional Analyses (per serving)

	BEFORE	AFTER		BEFORE	AFTER
Calories	620	292	Cholesterol	78 mg	43 mg
Protein	15 g	20 g	Fiber	N/A g	3 g
Carbohydrates	55 g	27 g	Sodium	1,290 mg	264 mg
Fat	38 g	11.5 g	% Calories from Fat	55	35
Saturated Fat	16 g	4 g	Omega-3 Fatty Acids	N/A	.2 g
Monounsaturated Fat	15 g	4.8 g	Omega-6 Fatty Acids	N/A	1.4 g
Polyunsaturated Fat	7 g	1.6 g			

Macaroni and Cheese

Makes 6 servings

You can serve this macaroni and cheese right after you stir the sauce and noodles together or you can spoon it into two loaf pans, sprinkle the top with crumbled croutons and paprika, and bake until it's bubbling and lightly browned around the edges. It's up to you. You can also serve one loaf pan and freeze the other for next week.

Canola oil cooking spray

2 cups [186 g] dry elbow macaroni

1 tablespoon [14 g] butter

¼ cup [61 g] fat-free or light sour cream

5 tablespoons [39 g] Wondra quick-mixing flour

2 cups [492 g] low-fat milk

1 cup [61 g] fat-free half-and-half

Salt and black pepper to taste

Pinch or two of cayenne pepper

3½ cups [396 g] shredded reduced-fat Cheddar cheese (substitute 1 cup [113 g] reduced-fat Monterey Jack or Gruyère cheese for some of the Cheddar, if desired)

⅔ cup [23 g] fat-free or regular croutons, crumbled (optional)

Paprika to taste

1. Preheat the oven to 350°F [180°C]. Coat two loaf pans (9 x 5-inch [23 x 13-cm]) with the cooking spray. Bring a large saucepan of lightly salted water to a boil. Add the macaroni and cook for 10 minutes or until al dente, then drain.

2. Meanwhile, in a medium-sized saucepan melt the butter, remove it from heat, and blend in the sour cream and flour to make a paste. Whisk in the milk and half-and-half and bring to a boil over medium heat, stirring frequently. Reduce the heat to simmer, stir in the salt, black pepper, and cayenne pepper, and stir frequently until the sauce thickens (about 5 minutes). Whisk in an additional tablespoon of flour if needed for desired thickness.

3. Remove the sauce from the heat, add the cheeses, and stir well. Pour the cheese sauce into a large saucepan, add the drained macaroni, and stir to combine. Serve immediately or pour the mixture into the prepared loaf pans. Sprinkle crumbled croutons and paprika (if desired). Bake for 30 minutes, or until the mixture bubbles and is lightly browned around the edges.

Nutritional Analyses (per serving)

	BEFORE	AFTER		BEFORE	AFTER
Calories	726	408	Cholesterol	170 mg	41 mg
Protein	28 g	27 g	Fiber	1.1 g	1 g
Carbohydrates	38 g	43.5 g	Sodium	648 mg	420 mg
Fat	49 g	13 g	% Calories from Fat	61	29
Saturated Fat	31 g	8 g	Omega-3 Fatty Acids	.5 g	.2 g
Monounsaturated Fat	14.5 g	3.7 g	Omega-6 Fatty Acids	.9 g	.5 g
Polyunsaturated Fat	1.4 g	.7 g			

Coq au Vin

Makes 6 servings

This is one of those hearty, satisfying dinners that are perfect for a cold winter night. The entrée begs to be served over egg noodles! You'll need about ¾ cup [120 g] of cooked noodles per serving. But even with the noodles or rice, each serving contains only 337 calories, and the fat content, too, is much lower than it is in traditional versions.

1 tablespoon [14 g] canola oil
4 skinless, boneless chicken breasts
4 skinless, boneless chicken thighs
½ cup [120 g] low-sodium chicken broth
Pinch or two of black pepper (optional)
12 shallots or pearl onions, peeled
1½ cups [144 g] whole button mushrooms
    (1½ cups [105 g] sliced mushrooms can
    be substituted)
1½ cups [227 g] baby carrots (1 cup [122 g]
    carrots, thinly sliced, can be substituted)
1¼ cups [37 g] Burgundy
1 tablespoon [4 g] finely chopped fresh
    parsley (or 1 teaspoon [.3 g] dried parsley)
2 teaspoons [6 g] minced or chopped garlic
½ teaspoon [.3 g] dried marjoram, crushed
½ teaspoon [.7 g] dried thyme, crushed
1 bay leaf
4 cups [640 g] cooked egg noodles or
    whole-wheat noodles (brown rice can be
    substituted)

SAUCE
2 tablespoons [16 g] Wondra quick-mixing
    flour (all-purpose flour can also be used)
2 tablespoons [30 g] fat-free sour cream
1 tablespoon [15 g] Burgundy
1 tablespoon [15 g] fat-free half-and-half
    or low-fat milk

1. Add the oil to a large nonstick skillet or saucepan and brown both sides of the chicken over medium heat (about 10 minutes). Add a tablespoon or two of chicken broth if needed for moisture. Sprinkle some pepper over the top, if desired.

2. Stir in the remaining chicken broth, and the shallots, mushrooms, carrots, Burgundy, parsley, garlic, marjoram, thyme, and bay leaf. Bring the mixture to a boil, reduce the heat to simmer, and cover the skillet. Simmer for about 40 minutes, or until the chicken is tender and cooked throughout. Remove the bay leaf and discard.

3. Place the cooked noodles on a serving platter. Remove the chicken and vegetables from the skillet with a slotted spoon and place them over the noodles. Cover and keep warm.

4. To make the sauce, combine the flour, sour cream, Burgundy, and half-and-half in a small bowl and stir to make a paste. Add the flour mixture to the skillet. Cook, stirring, over medium heat until the sauce thickens (about 5 minutes).

5. Pour the sauce over the chicken and vegetables and serve immediately.

Nutritional Analyses (per serving)

	BEFORE	AFTER		BEFORE	AFTER
Calories	553	337	Cholesterol	150 mg	122 mg
Protein	35 g	33 g	Fiber	2.6 g	2.6 g
Carbohydrates	34 g	34 g	Sodium	171 mg	113 mg
Fat	27 g	8 g	% Calories from Fat	44	19
Saturated Fat	8.5 g	1.6 g	Omega-3 Fatty Acids	.3 g	.3 g
Monounsaturated Fat	8 g	3.1 g	Omega-6 Fatty Acids	7.6 g	1.7 g
Polyunsaturated Fat	8 g	2.1 g			

Green Chile Chicken Enchilada Casserole

Makes 8 servings

I was thrilled when I served this lightened version to my own family because all of us enjoyed it, even the children. I cut the total fat and saturated fat in half and lowered the calories by about 150 per serving by doing a few simple things. I used skinless chicken, reduced-fat instead of regular Jack cheese, and fat-free instead of regular sour cream. I was also able to use 12 tortillas instead of the 18 called for in the original recipe.

Canola oil cooking spray

1 (32-ounce [907-g]) can green-chile enchilada sauce or bottled salsa verde

12 corn tortillas (torn into four pieces each)

4 cups [560 g] roasted skinless chicken breast, shredded (about 4 chicken breast halves)

1 cup [160 g] chopped onions

1 (8-ounce [227-g]) package reduced-fat Monterey Jack cheese, shredded (or a mixture of reduced-fat Jack and Cheddar cheeses)

8 ounces [227 g] fat-free sour cream (light sour cream can be substituted)

1. Preheat the oven to 350°F [180°C]. Coat a 9 x 13-inch [23 x 33-cm] baking dish with the cooking spray.

2. Pour about 1 cup [240 g] of the enchilada sauce into the bottom of the prepared baking dish. Arrange 4 tortillas (torn into pieces) in a single layer in the bottom of the dish. Top with half of the shredded chicken, half of the onions, one-third of the cheese, and ½ cup [121 g] of the sour cream. Use a spatula to spread the sour cream in the pan, then top with another cup of the enchilada sauce.

3. Repeat the layers, starting with the broken tortillas, then the remaining chicken, onions, another third of the cheese, and the remaining sour cream. Use a spatula to spread the sour cream and top with a cup of enchilada sauce.

4. Top with the remaining tortillas, enchilada sauce (about ¾ cup [180 g]), and cheese.

5. Coat one side of a sheet of aluminum foil with cooking spray and cover the dish with the foil (coated side down—this keeps the cheese from sticking to the foil) and bake for 45 minutes.

Nutritional Analyses (per serving)

	BEFORE	AFTER		BEFORE	AFTER
Calories	538	409	Cholesterol	117 mg	102 mg
Protein	33 g	35 g	Fiber	4.5 g	4.5 g
Carbohydrates	29 g	33 g	Sodium	395 mg	390 mg
Fat	33 g	15 g	% Calories from Fat	55	33
Saturated Fat	15 g	8.5 g	Omega-3 Fatty Acids	.4 g	.2 g
Monounsaturated Fat	10 g	3 g	Omega-6 Fatty Acids	5.2 g	1.3 g
Polyunsaturated Fat	6 g	1.5 g			

Stuffed Red Bell Peppers

Makes 3 stuffed peppers

These yummy, colorful peppers can be made to order. If you want to keep them vegetarian, leave out the sausage. If red bell peppers are too expensive, use green bell peppers. If you want to pump up the fiber and nutrients, use brown instead of white rice.

3 large red bell peppers (green, yellow, or orange can be substituted)

1 tablespoon [14 g] olive oil

1 cup [160 g] chopped onions

1 portabello mushroom, chopped (about 1 cup [70 g]) (crimini or white mushrooms can be substituted)

3 tablespoons [11 g] chopped fresh parsley

2 teaspoons [6 g] minced or chopped garlic

4 ounces (about ¾ cup [113 g]) light turkey polska kielbasa sausage, finely chopped (light sausage or superlean ground beef can be substituted)

1½ cups [293 g] cooked brown rice (white rice can be substituted)

½ teaspoon [1 g] paprika (add more to taste, if desired)

½ teaspoon [3 g] salt

½ teaspoon [3 g] freshly ground black pepper

⅛ teaspoon [pinch] ground allspice

1 cup [247 g] bottled marinara sauce (tomato sauce can be substituted)

¼ cup [28 g] grated reduced-fat sharp Cheddar cheese (optional)

1. Cut the top off the peppers (reserve the tops) and scoop out the seeds and the inside flesh. Discard the stems, but chop the pepper tops and set aside. Place the peppers on a large microwave-safe dish with about a cup of water in the bottom, cover, and microwave on high until just tender (about 8 minutes). Remove the peppers from the dish and set aside to cool.

2. Meanwhile, heat the oil in a small or medium-sized nonstick skillet over medium-high heat. Add the onions, mushroom, parsley, garlic, and reserved chopped pepper pieces. Sauté the mixture, stirring often, until the onions are soft (about 4 to 6 minutes). Spoon into a large bowl.

3. Add the kielbasa to the same skillet and cook over medium heat, crumbling the meat with the spatula as it cooks and is nicely browned (about 5 minutes). Add the meat to the onion mixture, then add the rice, paprika, salt, pepper, allspice, and ½ cup [125 g] of the marinara sauce. Stir to blend the ingredients well.

4. Fill the peppers with the rice mixture and stand the filled peppers in a loaf pan or similar deep dish and microwave on high for about 8 minutes. Pour the remaining marinara sauce evenly over the tops of the peppers and sprinkle with the Cheddar, if desired. Microwave, uncovered, for 2 to 3 minutes longer and serve.

Nutritional Analyses (per serving)

	BEFORE	AFTER		BEFORE	AFTER
Calories	491	354	Cholesterol	39 mg	20 mg
Protein	16 g	14 g	Fiber	8 g	9 g
Carbohydrates	48 g	55 g	Sodium	1,053 mg	1,043 mg
Fat	28 g	9.4 g	% Calories from Fat	51	24
Saturated Fat	7.5 g	2.5 g	Omega-3 Fatty Acids	.3 g	.1 g
Monounsaturated Fat	8.8 g	4 g	Omega-6 Fatty Acids	9.4 g	.9 g
Polyunsaturated Fat	10 g	1 g			

Smoked Scallop and Hazelnut Fettuccine

Makes 4 servings

This is one of those fancy recipes you make every once in a while because it's worth the extra effort—and the compliments heard across the dinner table. Once you get through the steps to "smoke" the nuts and scallops, you'll be home free. The original recipe called for a lot more butter and whipping cream.

1 cup water [237 g]

3 tablespoons [41 g] firmly packed brown sugar

2 tablespoons [37 g] kosher or coarse salt (table salt can be substituted)

1 teaspoon [5 g] liquid smoke (can be found in a small bottle in the barbecue section of the supermarket)

12 to 16 ounces [340 to 454 g] bay scallops, rinsed

½ cup [68 g] hazelnuts (macadamia nuts can be substituted)

Canola oil cooking spray

2 teaspoons [6 g] minced or chopped garlic

¾ cup [188 g] condensed chicken broth, divided

¾ cup [182 g] half-and-half

¾ cup [182 g] fat-free half-and-half (whole milk can also be used)

1 tablespoon [14 g] butter

10 to 12 ounces [284 to 340 g] fresh fettuccine noodles or 8 ounces [227 g] dry pasta

½ cup [40 g] shredded Parmesan cheese

⅓ cup [33 g] thinly sliced green onions (including tops)

1 tablespoon [3 g] chopped fresh dill or 1 teaspoon [1 g] dried dill weed

Freshly ground black pepper, to taste

1. In a measuring cup (or bowl), mix 1 cup [237 g] of water with 1½ tablespoons of the brown sugar, 1 tablespoon [18 g] of the salt, and ½ teaspoon [3 g] of the liquid smoke. Add the scallops; mix, cover, and chill for 30 minutes. Drain the scallops. (If you're making this up to a day ahead, cover and then chill overnight.)

2. In a 1-quart [1 l] saucepan, mix 1 cup [237 g] water with the remaining brown sugar, salt, and liquid smoke. Bring to a boil over high heat; add the hazelnuts, remove from the heat, and let stand for 30 minutes.

3. Preheat the oven to 325°F [170°C]. Drain the nuts, pat dry, and chop coarsely. Spread the nuts in a 9-inch [23-cm] pan and bake, shaking the pan occasionally, until they're golden brown (about 10 minutes). Pour the nuts into a small bowl. (If you're making this a day ahead, cover the nuts in an airtight container and store at room temperature.)

4. In a large nonstick skillet coated with the cooking spray, heat the garlic. Then add ¼ cup [63 g] of the chicken broth over high heat; stir often until the garlic is pale gold and the broth is almost gone (1 minute). Add all the half-and-half and the remaining chicken broth and bring to a boil over high heat; stir often for 2 to 3 minutes. Pour the mixture into a bowl. Rinse and dry the skillet and return it to high heat, adding the tablespoon of butter. As the butter melts, dry the scallops on paper towels. Add the scallops to the pan and gently cook until the juices have evaporated and the scallops are browned (about 6 minutes). Pour the cream mixture back into the skillet and stir to release the browned bits on the bottom; keep warm.

5. Meanwhile, bring about 3 quarts [2,844 g] of water to a boil. While the scallops are browning, add the pasta to the boiling water and cook until tender (3 to 4 minutes). Drain the pasta well and pour it into the scallop sauce; add the hazelnuts. Sprinkle with the Parmesan and then toss with two forks. Mount each serving of pasta on a dinner plate and sprinkle evenly with the green onions, dill, and pepper to taste, adding more Parmesan, as desired.

Nutritional Analyses (per serving)

	BEFORE	AFTER		BEFORE	AFTER
Calories	810	540	Cholesterol	171 mg	73 mg
Protein	34 g	36 g	Fiber	3.4 g	3 g
Carbohydrates	53 g	57 g	Sodium	520 mg	481 mg
Fat	52 g	18 g	% Calories from Fat	58	30
Saturated Fat	27 g	7.5 g	Omega-3 Fatty Acids	.7 g	.3 g
Monounsaturated Fat	19 g	8 g	Omega-6 Fatty Acids	2 g	.9 g
Polyunsaturated Fat	3 g	1.2 g			

Spinach and Prosciutto Lasagna

Makes 12 servings

The spinach in this version of lasagna appeals to the eye, while the sliced artichoke bottoms add a nice texture change. The Fontina-infused cheese sauce wakes up the taste buds, while the prosciutto is a pleasant surprise in each bite. The original recipe called for half-and-half; I used low-fat milk. The original recipe called for half a stick of butter. I used 1 tablespoon [14 g] of olive oil.

8 ounces [227 g] dried lasagna

1 tablespoon [14 g] olive or canola oil

1 onion, peeled and finely chopped (about 1 cup [160 g])

½ cup [63 g] Wondra quick-mixing flour

½ teaspoon [3 g] ground white pepper

¼ teaspoon [.5 g] ground nutmeg

4 cups [984 g] low-fat milk (whole or fat-free half-and-half can be substituted)

3 cups (12 ounces [324 g]) shredded Fontina cheese

Salt to taste

2 (14-ounce [397-g]) cans artichoke bottoms, drained

2 (10-ounce [284-g]) boxes frozen spinach, chopped and thawed

8 ounces [227 g] prosciutto or lean ham, thinly sliced

7 tablespoons [35 g] shredded Parmesan cheese

1. Preheat the oven to 375°F [190°C]. Bring 3 quarts [3 l] of water to a boil in a large nonstick saucepan. Add the lasagna and boil until barely tender (10 minutes). Drain the lasagna strips, immerse them in cold water to cool, and drain again.

2. In the same pan over medium-high heat, add the oil and onion and sauté, stirring often (about 5 minutes). Turn off the heat. Combine the flour, pepper, and nutmeg in a large measuring cup and stir in ¾ cup [177 ml] of the milk to make a paste. Add this to the onion mixture and immediately whisk in the remaining milk. Return to medium-high heat and whisk until the mixture boils and thickens (about 5 minutes). Reduce the heat and simmer, stirring often, for 5 minutes longer. Remove from the heat and add about 2 cups [216 g] of the Fontina, whisking until the cheese is melted and the sauce is smooth. Add salt to taste.

3. Rinse and drain the artichoke bottoms; cut the bottoms crosswise into ⅛-inch-thick [3-mm] slices. Squeeze as much liquid as possible from the spinach.

4. In a 9 x 13-inch [23 x 33-cm] baking dish, layer a third of the lasagna, half the artichoke bottoms, half the prosciutto, and half the spinach, spreading each layer level to the edges of the dish; spoon a third of the cheese sauce over the spinach and sprinkle with 2 tablespoons [10 g] of the Parmesan. Repeat the layer with lasagna, the remaining artichokes, prosciutto, and spinach, and pour half of the remaining cheese sauce over the spinach and sprinkle with 2 tablespoons [10 g] of the Parmesan. Cover with the remaining lasagna, cheese sauce, Fontina, and Parmesan.

5. Bake the lasagna, uncovered, until it is piping hot and lightly browned on top (about 35 minutes). Let stand for 10 minutes before serving.

Nutritional Analyses (per serving)

	BEFORE	AFTER		BEFORE	AFTER
Calories	470	335	Cholesterol	102 mg	55 mg
Protein	22 g	22 g	Fiber	2.5 g	4 g
Carbohydrates	30 g	31 g	Sodium	947 mg	940 mg
Fat	28 g	14 g	% Calories from Fat	54	38
Saturated Fat	16 g	7.3 g	Omega-3 Fatty Acids	.4 g	.3 g
Monounsaturated Fat	6.5 g	3.7 g	Omega-6 Fatty Acids	.5 g	.5 g
Polyunsaturated Fat	1 g	.8 g			

Ten-Minute Spaghetti Carbonara

Makes 4 servings

This dish is really easy to make using leftover spaghetti and it tastes so good—the perfect recipe for a busy weeknight. I used turkey bacon instead of the real deal, but if you're a bacon purist, try to use two strips instead of four.

4 cups [560 g] cooked spaghetti (until tender but still a little firm), drained

¼ cup [63 g] egg substitute

1 tablespoon [8 g] Wondra quick-mixing flour

½ cup plus 2 tablespoons [150 g] double-strength chicken broth (use reduced-sodium, if available)

¼ cup [59 g] dry white wine (champagne can be substituted)

2 tablespoons [28 g] butter

2 garlic cloves, minced (about 2 teaspoons [6 g])

Salt and freshly ground black pepper (optional)

4 slices turkey bacon, cooked and crumbled

⅔ cup [75 g] freshly grated Parmesan cheese

1. Cook the spaghetti according to the package directions. In a small bowl, blend the egg substitute with the flour and set aside.

2. In large nonstick skillet, combine the chicken broth, wine, butter, and garlic. Bring the mixture to a boil, and continue boiling gently for a minute or two. Turn off the heat. Season the mixture with salt and pepper, if desired.

3. Add the egg substitute mixture and stir well. Add the cooked spaghetti and toss well.

4. Stir in the bacon and the Parmesan and toss well.

Nutritional Analyses (per serving)

	BEFORE	AFTER		BEFORE	AFTER
Calories	552	370	Cholesterol	185 mg	38 mg
Protein	17 g	17 g	Fiber	2.4 g	2.5 g
Carbohydrates	42 g	42.5 g	Sodium	626 mg	536 mg
Fat	34 g	13 g	% Calories from Fat	55	32
Saturated Fat	19 g	7 g	Omega-3 Fatty Acids	.5 g	.2 g
Monounsaturated Fat	10.5 g	4 g	Omega-6 Fatty Acids	1.5 g	1.1 g
Polyunsaturated Fat	2 g	1.3 g			

Fettuccine Alfredo

Makes 4 servings

I know so many people who adore fettuccine Alfredo but can't order it in restaurants because it's too rich and heavy and can involve an entire week's worth of fat and calories in one meal! This is a creamy but light version that you can make at home without the guilt. If you really want to boost the nutrients and fiber in this dish, add some steamed broccoli or other vegetables.

1½ cups [366 g] whole milk, divided (fat-free half-and-half can be substituted)

¼ cup [60 g] light cream cheese

1 tablespoon [8 g] Wondra quick-mixing flour

2 tablespoons [28 g] butter (no- or low-trans margarine can be substituted)

6 cups [840 g] spaghetti or fettuccine, cooked and drained

Salt and black pepper to taste

Ground nutmeg to taste

Grated Parmesan cheese to taste

1. Combine ¼ cup [61 g] of the milk, the cream cheese, and flour in a small mixing bowl or a food processor. Beat or pulse until well blended. Slowly pour in the remaining milk and beat until smooth.

2. Melt the butter in a large, thick nonstick saucepan over medium heat. Add the milk mixture and continue to heat, stirring constantly, until the sauce has just thickened. Reduce the heat to low and add the hot pasta, tossing to coat well with the sauce. Add salt, pepper, and nutmeg to taste. Stir in the Parmesan and serve.

Nutritional Analyses (per serving)

	BEFORE	AFTER		BEFORE	AFTER
Calories	920	437	Cholesterol	90 mg	35 mg
Protein	23 g	15 g	Fiber	3 g	4 g
Carbohydrates	82 g	65 g	Sodium	1,270 mg	180 mg
Fat	55 g	12 g	% Calories from Fat	54	25
Saturated Fat	23 g	7.4 g	Omega-3 Fatty Acids	N/A	.2 g
Monounsaturated Fat	N/A	2.8 g	Omega-6 Fatty Acids	N/A	.7 g
Polyunsaturated Fat	N/A	.9 g			

Veggie Calzones

Makes 4 servings

Pizza is another notorious comfort food. In this more healthful rendition, I've turned pizza into a calzone, trading the higher-sodium, higher-fat toppings for higher-fiber vegetables, and switching to reduced-fat cheese and half whole-wheat flour for the crust. This recipe calls for a bread machine to make the calzone dough, but you can do it by hand—just mix the dough ingredients in a large bowl and knead the dough for 15 minutes. While the bread machine is kneading the dough, you can lightly cook the broccoli and pan-fry the eggplant.

DOUGH

1½ cups [188 g] bread flour or unbleached white flour (plus extra for rolling out the dough)

1½ cups [180 g] whole-wheat pastry flour

1⅛ cups [270 g] lukewarm water

2 tablespoons [25 g] sugar

1 tablespoon [14 g] olive oil

1½ teaspoons [6 g] rapid-rise or bread-machine yeast

1 teaspoon [6 g] salt

FILLING

Canola oil cooking spray

½ regular eggplant or 1 Japanese eggplant, sliced into ¼-inch-thick [6-mm] rounds

1½ cups [107 g] broccoli florets, chopped and lightly cooked in a microwave or steamer

1 cup [113 g] shredded part-skim mozzarella cheese

¼ cup [68 g] reduced-fat goat cheese, coarsely chopped

¼ cup [20 g] shredded Parmesan cheese

1 cup [40 g] fresh basil leaves

1 tablespoon [14 g] olive oil

Dash of red pepper flakes (optional)

1. To make the dough, place the flours, water, sugar, oil, yeast, and salt in the bread machine in the order recommended by the manufacturer. Set the bread machine on the dough cycle and press start.

2. Let the bread machine complete the mixing and kneading cycle (about 15 minutes). Unplug the machine and remove the dough from the pan. Let it rest on a lightly floured surface for 15 minutes. Divide it into 4 portions and let it rest for 10 minutes longer.

3. While the dough is being mixed, heat a large nonstick skillet over medium heat to make the filling. Generously coat the skillet with the cooking spray. Cover the bottom of the skillet with eggplant slices, spraying the tops with cooking spray. When the bottoms are lightly browned (about 3 minutes), flip them over, and brown the other side (3 minutes longer). Remove the eggplant slices from the skillet to cool.

4. Preheat the oven to 450°F [230°C]. Roll each portion of dough into a circle, and then stretch that into a circle 8 to 10 inches [20 to 25 cm] in diameter. Place the eggplant slices, broccoli, half of the mozzarella, and all of the goat cheese, Parmesan, and basil over half of all 4 of the dough circles (to make a semicircle). Top with the remaining mozzarella. Fold the dough over to form a half circle. Moisten the edges with water and crimp together. Place the calzones on a cookie sheet.

5. Combine the olive oil with the red pepper flakes (if desired) and brush the top surface of the dough with the mixture. Bake for 15 to 20 minutes, or until the calzones become crisp underneath and golden brown on top.

Nutritional Analyses (per serving)

	BEFORE	AFTER		BEFORE	AFTER
Calories	880	567	Cholesterol	83 mg	20 mg
Protein	35 g	26 g	Fiber	3 g	10 g
Carbohydrates	76 g	83 g	Sodium	1,772 mg	857 mg
Fat	50 g	15 g	% Calories from Fat	51	24
Saturated Fat	19 g	5.5 g	Omega-3 Fatty Acids	.5 g	.2 g
Monounsaturated Fat	25 g	7.3 g	Omega-6 Fatty Acids	3.5 g	.7 g
Polyunsaturated Fat	4 g	1 g			

Tasty Tofu Lasagna

Makes 4 servings

The tofu replaces the ricotta cheese in this lasagna recipe. You can also add some healthful veggies (try frozen chopped spinach, thinly sliced zucchini, grated carrot, finely diced eggplant, or any other veggie that sounds good). This recipe makes an 8 x 8-inch [20 x 20-cm] lasagna, but if you want a 9 x 13-inch [23 x 33-cm] lasagna just double all the ingredients.

Canola oil cooking spray

2½ cups [625 g] bottled marinara sauce, divided

6 oven-ready, no-boil lasagna strips

9 ounces [255 g] firm tofu, crumbled (about 1 cup [252 g])

2 tablespoons [30 g] fat-free half-and-half or low-fat milk

1 large egg

Pinch of black pepper

⅛ teaspoon [dash] ground nutmeg

1 cup [113 g] shredded part-skim mozzarella cheese, divided

1½ teaspoons [.5 g] dried parsley

1½ cups [123 g] raw veggie of choice (thinly sliced zucchini, grated carrot, diced eggplant, or 1 cup [156 g] thawed frozen chopped spinach)

¼ cup [20 g] shredded Parmesan cheese

1. Preheat the oven to 350°F [180°C]. Coat an 8 x 8-inch [20 x 20-cm] baking dish with the cooking spray.

2. Spread ½ cup [125 g] of the marinara sauce in the bottom of the baking dish. Lay two of the lasagna strips on top.

3. In a medium-sized bowl, combine the tofu, half-and-half, egg, pepper, and nutmeg. Add 1 cup [250 g] of the marinara sauce, ½ cup [57 g] of the mozzarella cheese, and the parsley. Spread half of this mixture on top of the lasagna strips, and top with half of the veggies.

4. Cover the veggies with two more lasagna strips, spread the remaining tofu mixture on top, and follow with the remainder of the veggies.

5. Cover the veggies with the last two lasagna strips and spread the remaining marinara sauce on top. Sprinkle with the remaining mozzarella and end with the Parmesan.

6. Cover the dish with aluminum foil and bake for about 30 minutes. Remove the foil and bake for about 5 minutes longer to lightly brown the top of the lasagna before serving.

Nutritional Analyses (per serving)

	BEFORE	AFTER		BEFORE	AFTER
Calories	675	383	Cholesterol	100 mg	72 mg
Protein	40 g	24 g	Fiber	5 g	5 g
Carbohydrates	69 g	49 g	Sodium	674 mg	764 mg
Fat	27 g	10 g	% Calories from Fat	36	23
Saturated Fat	14 g	5 g	Omega-3 Fatty Acids	.2 g	.4 g
Monounsaturated Fat	9 g	2.6 g	Omega-6 Fatty Acids	1.2 g	.6 g
Polyunsaturated Fat	1.5 g	1.4 g			

Sugo Bianco Pasta

Makes 5 servings

This is a light remake of a popular chicken and pasta dish. The heavier, calorie-laden version can be found at the Macaroni Grill, an Italian-themed restaurant chain.

SAUCE
2 cups [484 g] fat-free half-and-half
2 cups [488 g] whole milk
1 cup [113 g] shredded Asiago cheese
1 teaspoon [6 g] low-sodium chicken-broth powder
1 tablespoon [8 g] cornstarch
1½ tablespoons [22 g] cold water

PASTA
1 tablespoon [14 g] butter
½ cup [80 g] chopped red onion
½ cup [68 g] chopped pancetta (optional)
1 tablespoon [9 g] chopped garlic
6 cups [840 g] cooked farfalle (bowtie pasta), drained
2 cups [280 g] roasted or grilled chicken breast, shredded
¾ cup [75 g] thinly sliced green onions (green part only)
1 tablespoon [4 g] finely chopped fresh parsley

1. To make the sauce, heat the half-and-half and whole milk over medium-high heat in a nonstick medium-sized saucepan until it bubbles (about 4 minutes). Add the Asiago and chicken-broth powder. Stir constantly with a wire whisk and bring the temperature back to just bubbling (about 1 minute).

2. In a small cup, dissolve the cornstarch in cold water to make a thin paste and stir this into the cheese sauce. Bring the sauce to a simmer over low heat and stir for about 4 minutes. You can transfer the sauce to a covered container and refrigerate until needed, if desired.

3. For the pasta part of the dish, melt the butter in a large nonstick skillet over medium heat and sauté the onion for about 30 seconds. Stir in the pancetta (if desired) and garlic and sauté for another minute. Stir in the cooked pasta, chicken, and green onions and continue to cook, tossing the mixture, for another minute or two. Pour in the cheese sauce and stir to combine and heat the mixture thoroughly. (This will take a few minutes longer if the cheese sauce has been in the refrigerator.) Sprinkle the parsley over the pasta and serve.

Nutritional Analyses (per serving)

	BEFORE	AFTER		BEFORE	AFTER
Calories	990	595	Cholesterol	263 mg	92 mg
Protein	36 g	42 g	Fiber	3.5 g	3.5 g
Carbohydrates	58 g	67 g	Sodium	573 mg	472 mg
Fat	67 g	16 g	% Calories from Fat	61	24
Saturated Fat	39 g	8.5 g	Omega-3 Fatty Acids	.5 g	.3 g
Monounsaturated Fat	17 g	4 g	Omega-6 Fatty Acids	2.5 g	1.8 g
Polyunsaturated Fat	3 g	2.2 g			

Spicy Chicken Linguine

Makes 4 servings

If you don't like spicy foods, you can still enjoy this wonderful dish—simply use Mrs. Dash Extra Spicy instead of the crushed red pepper. This will give it just enough flavor without tons of heat. The original recipe contained a lot more butter, Parmesan, real sour cream, and chicken with the skin.

2 tablespoons [28 g] butter (no- or low-trans margarine can be substituted)

¼ cup [61 g] fat-free or light sour cream

½ cup [126 g] double-strength or concentrated chicken broth

1 medium onion, thinly sliced

1 tablespoon [2 g] dried basil (2 teaspoons [4 g] of Italian herbs can be substituted)

1½ teaspoons [4 g] minced or chopped garlic

½ teaspoon [1 g] crushed red pepper (1 teaspoon [2 g] Mrs. Dash Extra Spicy can be substituted)

4 skinless and boneless chicken breast halves

4 cups [560 g] cooked linguine, spaghetti, or angel hair pasta

1 box (10 ounces [283 g]) frozen spinach, chopped, thawed, and squeezed gently of excess liquid

¾ cup [60 g] shredded or grated Parmesan cheese

Salt and black pepper to taste (optional)

1. Preheat the oven to 350°F [180°C]. Add the butter to a 9 x 13-inch [23 x 33-cm] baking pan and place the pan in the oven to melt the butter (about 2 minutes). Stir in the sour cream using a fork. Slowly stir in the chicken broth. Then stir in the onion slices, basil, garlic, and red pepper.

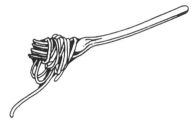

2. Coat both sides of the chicken breasts in the butter-spice mixture and spread them out evenly in the pan, placing some onion slices over each breast.

3. Cover the pan with aluminum foil and bake for 45 minutes. Meanwhile, boil the linguine until just tender.

4. After the chicken breasts have been cooked throughout (about 45 minutes), remove them from the pan and place them temporarily on a plate. Add the linguine, spinach, and Parmesan to the pan and toss to stir everything well. Add salt and pepper to taste, if desired.

5. Place the chicken on top of the pasta and spinach mixture (sprinkle additional grated Parmesan over the top, if desired) and bake for an additional 5 to 10 minutes. Serve!

Nutritional Analyses (per serving)

	BEFORE	AFTER		BEFORE	AFTER
Calories	739	500	Cholesterol	164 mg	100 mg
Protein	47 g	43 g	Fiber	4.5 g	4.6 g
Carbohydrates	46 g	48 g	Sodium	886 mg	625 mg
Fat	40 g	14 g	% Calories from Fat	49	25
Saturated Fat	22 g	7.5 g	Omega-3 Fatty Acids	.6 g	.3 g
Monounsaturated Fat	12.5 g	4.3 g	Omega-6 Fatty Acids	2.5 g	1.2 g
Polyunsaturated Fat	3.3 g	1.5 g			

Quick Kielbasa Macaroni and Cheese

Makes 4 servings

Macaroni and cheese from a box is comfort food to people who grew up with the familiar blue-and-orange box. So here's a macaroni and cheese casserole using that same boxed macaroni and cheese. I altered the directions on the box, however, to cut down on calories and reduce fat grams by more than half. Using a less-fat turkey polska kielbasa sausage helps shave off even more calories and fat.

Canola oil cooking spray

1 small box macaroni and cheese (with cheese packet)

¼ cup [61 g] low-fat milk or fat-free half-and-half

2 tablespoons [28 g] no- or low-trans margarine or butter

8 ounces [227 g] (about ½ package) turkey polska kielbasa sausage, sliced diagonally

¾ cup [135 g] diced tomato

¼ cup [25 g] chopped green onions

1. Preheat the oven to 400°F [200°C]. Coat an 8 x 8-inch [20 x 20-cm] or 9 x 9-inch [23 x 23-cm] baking dish with the cooking spray.

2. Boil 6 cups of water. Pour in the macaroni from the box and boil for 7 to 10 minutes until tender, stirring occasionally. Drain the macaroni well and return it to the pot.

3. Add the milk, margarine, and cheese-sauce packet and mix well.

4. Heat a large nonstick skillet over medium-high heat and cook the kielbasa slices until they're lightly browned on both sides.

5. Stir the kielbasa slices into the macaroni and cheese mixture, along with the tomato and green onions. Spoon the mixture into the prepared dish and bake for 15 to 20 minutes. Serve.

Nutritional Analyses (per serving)

	BEFORE	AFTER		BEFORE	AFTER
Calories	496	320	Cholesterol	78 mg	45 mg
Protein	17 g	18 g	Fiber	2 g	2 g
Carbohydrates	41 g	41.5 g	Sodium	1,160 mg	984 mg
Fat	29.5 g	9 g	% Calories from Fat	54	25
Saturated Fat	14.5 g	3.5 g	Omega-3 Fatty Acids	N/A	N/A
Monounsaturated Fat	11 g	2.8 g	Omega-6 Fatty Acids	N/A	N/A
Polyunsaturated Fat	2.3 g	2.2 g			

Chicken-Pesto Lasagna

Makes 12 servings

Tired of the same old lasagna? I actually served this at my wedding reception, and to this day it remains one of my favorite dinners. This lasagna is lighter than most because it includes skinless chicken breasts, part-skim ricotta cheese, part-skim mozzarella cheese, a nice, low-fat bottled marinara sauce, and no additional cooking fat. I used a store-bought pesto sauce, though, which adds some olive oil, and I used some Parmesan cheese as well, but I consider those fat grams to be well spent. You can save time making this recipe by buying roasted chicken breasts from your supermarket or rotisserie restaurant and using no-boil lasagna.

4 skinless, boneless chicken breasts, cut into bite-size pieces

1 packet low-sodium chicken broth mixed with ¾ cup [178 g] water

2 teaspoons [4 g] Italian seasonings

2 cups [248 g] grated zucchini

⅔ cup (5 ounces [188 g]) pesto

1½ cups [369 g] part-skim ricotta cheese

⅔ cup [75 g] chopped green onions

½ cup [40 g] grated Parmesan cheese

12 ounces (dry weight [340 g]) lasagna strips (a 9-ounce [255-g] box of no-boil lasagna can be substituted)

1 bottle (26 to 28 ounces [737 to 794 g]) marinara sauce

8 ounces (2 cups [227 g]) grated or shredded part-skim mozzarella cheese

Canola or olive oil cooking spray

1. Preheat the oven to 375°F [190°C]. In a skillet, simmer the chicken pieces in the broth mixture and Italian seasonings over medium heat until cooked throughout. Using a slotted spoon, remove the chicken from the skillet. Lightly shred the chicken in a food processor, adding the zucchini and pesto.

2. In a medium-sized bowl, combine the ricotta cheese, green onions, and Parmesan and mix well.

3. Cook the lasagna until just tender (following the package directions if necessary) and drain well.

4. To assemble the lasagna: Spread 1 cup [250 g] of marinara sauce on the bottom of a 9 x 13-inch [23 x 33-cm] baking pan. Add three strips of lasagna. Spread half of the chicken mixture on top. Add three more lasagna strips and spread all of the cheese mixture on top. Add three more strips of lasagna, and top with the rest of the chicken mixture. Add the last three lasagna strips. Spread the remaining marinara sauce on top and sprinkle evenly with the mozzarella cheese.

5. Coat one side of a sheet of aluminum foil with the cooking spray and cover the lasagna, sprayed side of the foil (the spray keeps the top from sticking to the cheese). Bake for 25 minutes. Remove the foil and bake for 10 minutes longer, or until the top is lightly golden and the sauce is bubbling.

Nutritional Analyses (per serving)

	BEFORE	AFTER		BEFORE	AFTER
Calories	370	338	Cholesterol	44 mg	49 mg
Protein	17 g	25 g	Fiber	1.8 g	3 g
Carbohydrates	35 g	31 g	Sodium	723 mg	490 mg
Fat	18.5 g	12 g	% Calories from Fat	45	32
Saturated Fat	9 g	5.3 g	Omega-3 Fatty Acids	N/A	.2 g
Monounsaturated Fat	N/A	3.3 g	Omega-6 Fatty Acids	N/A	.8 g
Polyunsaturated Fat	N/A	1 g			

Mushroom Penne Pasta

Makes 4 servings

This recipe calls for 2 tablespoons [28 g] of butter for browning the mushrooms and onion. The butter is indespensible because, when it browns, it produces more than a hundred different flavor components, many of which impart a rich taste to the dish.

1½ cups [107 g] broccoli florets

⅓ cup [48 g] frozen petite green peas

2 tablespoons [28 g] butter

2 cups [140 g] sliced brown crimini
   mushrooms (with stems removed)

½ cup [80 g] chopped sweet onion

1½ teaspoons [4 g] minced or chopped garlic

½ cup [121 g] half-and-half

½ cup [121 g] fat-free half-and-half

6 cups [690 g] cooked penne pasta, drained

⅓ cup [33 g] freshly grated or shredded
   Parmesan cheese

Salt and black pepper to taste

1. Place the broccoli florets and peas in a microwave-safe dish and microwave on high for 3 minutes or until lightly cooked; drain and set aside.

2. Melt the butter in a medium-sized nonstick skillet over medium heat. Add the mushrooms and onion, stir, and sauté for about 4 minutes. Keep the skillet covered, stirring every minute or so.

3. Stir in the garlic, cover, and sauté for another minute or until the mixture is lightly browned. Reduce the heat to low and stir in the broccoli, peas, all the half-and-half, and the pasta. Toss and cook for about a minute, stirring constantly.

4. Sprinkle the Parmesan over the pasta. Add salt and pepper to taste and serve.

Nutritional Analyses (per serving)

	BEFORE	AFTER		BEFORE	AFTER
Calories	684	479	Cholesterol	119 mg	36 mg
Protein	18 g	19 g	Fiber	5 g	5 g
Carbohydrates	69 g	72 g	Sodium	333 mg	247 mg
Fat	38 g	12 g	% Calories from Fat	50	22
Saturated Fat	23 g	7 g	Omega-3 Fatty Acids	.6 g	.2 g
Monounsaturated Fat	11 g	3.4 g	Omega-6 Fatty Acids	1.4 g	.7 g
Polyunsaturated Fat	2 g	1 g			

Crab Casserole

Makes 4 to 6 servings

For those of you who like your crab served as part of a creamy casserole this recipe is for you! The original recipe used half-and-half and real mayonnaise. I used fat-free half-and-half, only a few tablespoons of light mayonnaise, and some fat-free sour cream to make up the difference.

Canola oil cooking spray
2 large eggs, hard-boiled and cooled
1 cup [242 g] fat-free half-and-half
3 tablespoons [42 g] light mayonnaise
½ cup [121 g] fat-free sour cream
2 green onions, finely chopped
1 tablespoon [4 g] finely chopped fresh parsley
    or 1 teaspoon [pinch] dried parsley

¼ teaspoon [1 g] Old Bay seasoning
¼ cup [61 g] dry sherry
1½ cups [300 g] herb-seasoned dry bread
    stuffing
½ pound [227 g] cooked crabmeat

1. Preheat the oven to 400°F [200°C]. Coat an 8 x 8-inch [20 x 20-cm] baking dish with the cooking spray.

2. Shell the hard-boiled eggs, discard one of the yolks, and chop the remaining egg and egg white.

3. In a large bowl, combine the chopped eggs, half-and-half, mayonnaise, sour cream, green onions, parsley, Old Bay seasoning, and sherry. Stir in the bread stuffing and crabmeat.

4. Spoon the mixture into the prepared baking dish and bake for 30 to 40 minutes, or until bubbly and slightly browned on top.

Nutritional Analyses (per serving)

	BEFORE	AFTER		BEFORE	AFTER
Calories	536	265	Cholesterol	209 mg	114 mg
Protein	20 g	22 g	Fiber	1.3 g	1.3 g
Carbohydrates	20.5 g	25 g	Sodium	702 mg	621 mg
Fat	40.5 g	6.5 g	% Calories from Fat	68	22
Saturated Fat	10 g	1.4 g	Omega-3 Fatty Acids	4 g	.9 g
Monounsaturated Fat	12 g	1.5 g	Omega-6 Fatty Acids	9 g	1.2 g
Polyunsaturated Fat	16 g	3 g			

Taco Casserole

Makes 6 servings

This casserole a sure crowd-pleaser—great to make for parties or buffets.

1 pound [454 g] superlean ground beef or
  ground sirloin
1 package taco seasoning
¾ cup [178 g] nonalcoholic beer or water
1 (16-ounce [426-g]) can fat-free or
  vegetarian refried beans
¾ cup [120 g] chopped onion
1 cup [113 g] shredded reduced-fat
  Monterey Jack and sharp Cheddar cheese

6 ounces [170 g] low-fat or reduced-fat
  tortilla chips (or similar),
  coarsely crumbled
6 cups [336 g] shredded romaine lettuce
1 cup [242 g] fat-free sour cream
½ cup [125 g] salsa of your choice
1 avocado, peeled, seeded, and cut into
  wedges or diced (optional)

1. Preheat the oven to 375°F [190°C].

2. In a large nonstick skillet, brown the ground beef over medium heat, breaking the meat into very small pieces. Mix the taco seasoning and beer into the beef and continue to cook for a minute ot two.

3. Spread the beans on the bottom of a 9 x 13-inch [23 x 33-cm] baking dish. Spread the beef over the top and add the chopped onion. Sprinkle with the cheese and tortilla chips and bake for 20 minutes, or until the casserole is hot throughout.

4. Serve over a bed of lettuce and garnish with sour cream, salsa, and avocado, if desired.

Nutritional Analyses (per serving)

	BEFORE	AFTER		BEFORE	AFTER
Calories	566	398	Cholesterol	89 mg	57 mg
Protein	29 g	30 g	Fiber	8 g	9 g
Carbohydrates	41 g	51 g	Sodium	1,087 mg	1,103 mg
Fat	32 g	9 g	% Calories from Fat	51	20
Saturated Fat	15 g	4.4 g	Omega-3 Fatty Acids	1 g	1 g
Monounsaturated Fat	9 g	1.7 g	Omega-6 Fatty Acids	1 g	1 g
Polyunsaturated Fat	2 g	2 g			

Day After Thanksgiving Sheperd's Pie

Makes 6 servings

This is a wonderful way to enjoy leftover turkey, mashed potatoes, green vegetables, and gravy.

Canola oil cooking spray

⅔ cup [120 g] chopped mild or sweet onion

2 cups [280 g] diced roasted turkey breast

2 cups [466 g] leftover (or bottled) gravy (see light recipe on page 105)

2 cups [364 g] assorted leftover vegetables (green beans, carrots, peas)

½ to 1 teaspoon [3 to 6 g] Worcestershire sauce

2 cups [420 g] mashed potatoes (see light recipe on page 104)

1 tablespoon [15 g] fat-free half-and-half or low-fat milk

Freshly ground black pepper

1. Preheat the oven to 400°F [200°C]. Coat a deep-dish pie plate with the cooking spray.

2. Coat a large nonstick skillet with the cooking spray, add the onion, and cook until the onion is lightly browned. Stir in the turkey, gravy, vegetables, and Worcestershire sauce.

3. Spread the turkey mixture in the prepared pie plate. Spread the mashed potatoes over the meat. With a fork, make a crosshatch design in the mashed potatoes.

4. With a pastry brush, brush the top of the potatoes with the half-and-half. Sprinkle with black pepper, if desired.

5. Place the dish in the oven and cook until the pie is golden on top (about 25 minutes).

Nutritional Analyses (per serving)

	BEFORE	AFTER		BEFORE	AFTER
Calories	276	244	Cholesterol	43 mg	38 mg
Protein	15 g	20 g	Fiber	5 g	5 g
Carbohydrates	27 g	28 g	Sodium	938 mg	700 mg
Fat	13 g	6 g	% Calories from Fat	42	22
Saturated Fat	5 g	2 g	Omega-3 Fatty Acids	.2 g	.1 g
Monounsaturated Fat	4.5 g	2 g	Omega-6 Fatty Acids	2.4 g	1.1 g
Polyunsaturated Fat	3 g	1.2 g			

Corned Beef, Potatoes, and Cabbage

Makes 4 large servings

What I love about this recipe is that it involves just four easy ingredients: corned beef with its seasoning packet, a few potatoes, a small head of cabbage, and a bottle of nonalcoholic beer. The one thing I do to make this dish more healthful is trim all visible fat from the brisket. What's left is the mostly protein, flavorful portion of the corned beef. And since there's no visible fat on the brisket, there's practically no fat melting into the broth—so you can happily enjoy a big spoonful of broth poured over your portion of corned beef, potatoes, and cabbage.

2½ pounds [1.13 kg] boneless corned beef brisket (approximately) with seasoning packet

3 large potatoes, peeled and cut into chunks

1 (12-ounce [4,248-g]) bottle nonalcoholic beer

1 small head of cabbage, shredded or cut into ⅓-inch [8-mm] slices

1. Trim the brisket of all visible fat and remove the seasoning packet from the package.

2. Place the brisket in the bottom of a slow cooker and sprinkle the seasonings from the packet evenly over the top.

3. Spread the potatoes evenly over the top of the brisket and pour the beer over the potatoes. Cover the slow cooker, set it on low, and let it cook for about 7 hours. After about 4 to 5 hours, you can spoon some of the broth in the bottom of the slow cooker over the potatoes, if desired.

4. About an hour before you serve the dish (or after 7 hours of cooking), place the shredded cabbage over the top of the potatoes, cover again, and cook for an hour or so longer, or until the cabbage is just tender.

5. Serve this dish in individual soup dishes—with each serving getting a nice chunk of the corned beef, plenty of potatoes and cabbage, and a spoonful of broth ladled over the top.

Nutritional Analyses (per serving)

	BEFORE	AFTER		BEFORE	AFTER
Calories	600	476	Cholesterol	102 mg	50 mg
Protein	34 g	35 g	Fiber	7 g	7 g
Carbohydrates	48 g	48 g	Sodium	1,000 mg	1,000 mg
Fat	29 g	16 g	% Calories from Fat	44	30
Saturated Fat	12 g	6 g	Omega-3 Fatty Acids	.4 g	.3 g
Monounsaturated Fat	13.5 g	9 g	Omega-6 Fatty Acids	.8 g	.6 g
Polyunsaturated Fat	1.2 g	1 g			

Pasta with Four-Cheese Sauce

Makes 4 to 6 servings

This is a lower-fat and lower-calorie way to prepare a fancy cheese sauce to top your favorite pasta. Serve it as a side dish with your favorite grilled fish.

4 cups [420 g] dry pasta (penne, mostaccioli, or rotelle)

2 tablespoons [16 g] Wondra quick-mixing flour

⅔ cup [185 g] low-fat milk (whole milk can be substituted)

½ cup [54 g] grated reduced-fat Swiss cheese

¼ cup [25 g] grated Parmesan cheese

4 ounces [113 g] light cream cheese

1½ ounces (3 tablespoons [43 g]) blue cheese

1 teaspoon [3 g] minced garlic

White or black pepper to taste

1. Cook the pasta in lightly salted boiling water until just tender (about 10 minutes). Drain and set aside.

2. Add the flour to a small nonstick saucepan. Slowly pour in ¼ cup [62 g] of the milk and stir until smooth. Slowly pour in the remaining milk while stirring. Heat the mixture over medium-low heat, stirring constantly, until the sauce begins to thicken (about 2 minutes).

3. Add the cheeses and the garlic to the milk mixture. Continue to cook over low heat, stirring constantly, until all ingredients are melted and the mixture is reasonably smooth. If it is too thick, add a tablespoon or two of milk and stir. Add white or black pepper to taste.

4. Toss the sauce with the cooked pasta and serve.

Nutritional Analyses (per serving)

	BEFORE	AFTER		BEFORE	AFTER
Calories	431	374	Cholesterol	50 mg	22 mg
Protein	16 g	17 g	Fiber	1.7 g	1.7 g
Carbohydrates	54 g	55 g	Sodium	234 mg	245 mg
Fat	16 g	8.5 g	% Calories from Fat	33	20
Saturated Fat	10 g	5.3 g	Omega-3 Fatty Acids	.2 g	.1 g
Monounsaturated Fat	4.3 g	.8 g	Omega-6 Fatty Acids	.7 g	.4 g
Polyunsaturated Fat	.9 g	.5 g			

CHAPTER FOUR

One-Dish Wonders
(or Soups and Stews)

Hot and savory, these favorite soups and stews swim circles around store-bought canned options. Not only are these recipes lightened for calories and fat but the prep time has been shaved off, too. Try this timesaving tip: Make a batch on the weekend and freeze half of the recipe for a quick weeknight meal later in the week.

Grand-Prize Chili

Makes 4 servings

Chili is one of America's favorite meals. Served with warm corn bread, it really hits the spot.

2 teaspoons [9 g] canola oil

1 pound [454 g] beef top round (such as London broil), trimmed of fat and cut into ¼-inch cubes [6-mm]

1 onion, finely chopped

3 garlic cloves, minced or pressed

1 (15-ounce [425-g]) can low-sodium kidney beans (or pinto beans), drained and rinsed

1 (14½-ounce [411-g]) can Mexican-style stewed tomatoes

1 cup [237 g] light or nonalcoholic beer or water

2 to 3 teaspoons [5 to 8 g] chili powder

1 teaspoon [2 g] paprika

1 teaspoon [2 g] ground cumin

1 teaspoon [2 g] dried oregano

⅓ to ½ jalapeño pepper, halved, seeded and finely chopped (optional)

1 onion, finely minced, for serving (optional)

Grated reduced-fat sharp Cheddar or Monterey Jack cheese (optional)

1. Heat the oil over medium-high heat in a large nonstick skillet. Add the beef, onion, and garlic, stirring occasionally, until browned (about 3 minutes).

2. Spoon the beef mixture into a slow cooker. Add the beans, tomatoes (including liquid), beer, chili powder, paprika, cumin, oregano, and jalapeño, if desired. Stir to combine. Cover and turn the slow cooker on low. Cook for 8 to 10 hours.

3. Serve in small bowls, sprinkling each with the onion and grated cheese, if desired.

Nutritional Analyses (per serving)

	BEFORE	AFTER		BEFORE	AFTER
Calories	493	364	Cholesterol	55 mg	76 mg
Protein	28 g	38 g	Fiber	10 g	10 g
Carbohydrates	33 g	31.5 g	Sodium	750 mg	431 mg
Fat	26 g	8 g	% Calories from Fat	47	20
Saturated Fat	8.5 g	2.2 g	Omega-3 Fatty Acids	.4 g	.4 g
Monounsaturated Fat	10 g	3.5 g	Omega-6 Fatty Acids	4.5 g	.8 g
Polyunsaturated Fat	5 g	1.2 g			

Irish Chicken and Dumplings

Makes 8 hearty servings

Traditional chicken and dumplings is Irish comfort food at its best. Here is the lighter version.

2 (10¾-ounce [318-ml]) cans reduced-fat condensed cream of chicken soup

3 cups [711 g] water

2 medium onions, coarsely chopped

1 cup [120 g] sliced or chopped celery

½ teaspoon [3 g] salt (optional)

½ teaspoon [3 g] poultry seasoning

½ teaspoon [3 g] freshly ground black pepper

4 skinless, boneless chicken breast halves

4 whole carrots, sliced (about 4 cups [512 g])

2 large potatoes, peel and cut into ½-inch [13-mm] slices then quartered

½ cup [72 g] frozen green peas

1½ cups [188 g] reduced-fat Bisquick baking mix

⅓ cup [81 g] low-fat buttermilk

⅓ cup [80 g] fat-free half-and-half or low-fat milk

1. In a large saucepan, combine the soup, water, onions, celery, salt (if desired), poultry seasoning, and pepper. Add the chicken breasts, carrots, and potatoes. Bring to a boil, reduce to a simmer, and cover the pan. Simmer over low heat for approximately 30 minutes.

2. Remove the chicken from the saucepan, shred it into bite-size pieces (or break it up into pieces in the saucepan using a spatula), and return it to the saucepan and stir in the peas.

3. Combine the Bisquick, buttermilk, and half-and-half in a medium-sized bowl and blend to make a dough. Drop the dough by spoonfuls into the stew. Cover the pan and simmer for about 20 minutes. Uncover the pan and simmer for 10 minutes longer. Serve hot.

Nutritional Analyses (per serving)

	BEFORE	AFTER		BEFORE	AFTER
Calories	426	349	Cholesterol	57 mg	43 mg
Protein	22 g	21 g	Fiber	5 g	5 g
Carbohydrates	51 g	54 g	Sodium	976 mg	648 mg
Fat	15 g	4.5 g	% Calories from Fat	32	12
Saturated Fat	5 g	1.5 g	Omega-3 Fatty Acids	.06 g	.2 g
Monounsaturated Fat	5 g	1 g	Omega-6 Fatty Acids	.8 g	.6 g
Polyunsaturated Fat	3 g	1 g			

Pasta e Fagioli

Makes about 8 servings

I used a superlean ground beef in this soup, some canned kidney and white beans, which give a big boost to the fiber, and as many veggies as would fit into the soup pot. I also made low-sodium choices throughout this soup chapter to help those who are on a low-sodium diet. If this isn't a concern for you, you can either add salt to taste at the end or use the regular sodium products when making the soup.

2 cups [210 g] small (about ⅓ inch [8 mm]) dry pasta (such as pipette)

1 pound [454 g] superlean ground beef or ground sirloin

1 cup [160 g] chopped onions

1 tablespoon [9 g] minced or chopped garlic

1 cup [120 g] sliced celery stalks

1 cup [128 g] diced carrots (regular or baby carrots)

2 (14½-ounce [411-g]) cans diced Italian tomatoes (low-sodium, if available)

1 (15-ounce [425-g]) can white beans (or similar), rinsed and drained

1 (15-ounce [425-g]) can red kidney beans, rinsed and drained

1 (15-ounce [425-g]) can low-sodium tomato sauce

2 (5½-ounce [162-ml]) cans V8 juice (lower-sodium, if available)

3 cups [720 g] low-sodium beef, chicken, or vegetable broth

1 tablespoon [15 g] white or rice vinegar

½ teaspoon [pinch] dried thyme

½ teaspoon [3 g] black pepper

1 teaspoon [1 g] dried basil

1 teaspoon [1 g] dried oregano

About ½ cup [40 g] shredded or grated Parmesan cheese (optional)

1. Bring a large saucepan half filled with water to a rolling boil. Add the pasta and follow the directions on the package to cook al dente. Drain and set aside.

2. While the pasta is boiling, you can brown the ground beef in a large nonstick saucepan over medium-high heat. When the beef is almost cooked throughout, add the onions, garlic, celery, and carrots to the beef. Stir the mixture and let it cook for about 5 minutes.

3. Add all the remaining ingredients (not including the pasta and the Parmesan), stir the mixture, cover the saucepan, and lower the heat to simmer. Simmer for about 45 minutes. Stir in the cooked pasta and continue to simmer for about 15 minutes or until you're ready to serve. Sprinkle about 1 tablespoon of the Parmesan over each bowl of soup, if desired.

Nutritional Analyses (per serving)

	BEFORE	AFTER		BEFORE	AFTER
Calories	424	337	Cholesterol	37 mg	30 mg
Protein	23 g	24 g	Fiber	10 g	10 g
Carbohydrates	54 g	54 g	Sodium	1,537 mg	877 mg
Fat	14.5 g	4 g	% Calories from Fat	30	11
Saturated Fat	4 g	1.3 g	Omega-3 Fatty Acids	.2 g	.1 g
Monounsaturated Fat	4.9 g	1.3 g	Omega-6 Fatty Acids	3.5 g	.4 g
Polyunsaturated Fat	3.7 g	.7 g			

Light French Onion Soup with Soup Croutons

Makes 6 servings

To make this soup even better, I've topped each bowl with some grated reduced-fat Jarlsberg or Swiss cheese. Broil it until the top gets bubbly.

4 tablespoons [20 g] shredded Parmesan cheese

3 ounces [85 g] shredded reduced-fat Jarlsberg or Swiss cheese

1 tablespoon [14 g] olive oil

4 large yellow onions, thinly sliced lengthwise

1 tablespoon [9 g] minced garlic

2 bay leaves

1 (12-ounce [354-g]) bottle nonalcoholic or light beer

½ teaspoon [3 g] salt (optional)

½ teaspoon [3 g] freshly ground black pepper

¼ cup [59 g] Madeira (or similar)

2 cups [480 g] low-sodium chicken or beef broth

1 (10½-ounce [310-ml]) can condensed beef consommé

Soup croutons (recipe follows)

1. Combine the cheeses in a bowl and set aside. Heat the olive oil in a nonstick soup pot or saucepan over medium-low heat. Add the onions, garlic, and bay leaves and cook until the onions brown.

2. Add ½ cup [118 g] of the beer and cook until the onions caramelize. Add the salt and pepper and continue stirring for another minute. Add the Maderia and the remaining beer and cook until the liquid is reduced by half. Add the broth and consommé, cover, and simmer for 30 minutes. Adjust the seasoning, if necessary, and remove the bay leaves.

3. Preheat the broiler. Ladle the soup into ovenproof bowls, float 1 crouton in each, and sprinkle with the cheese mixture. Set the bowls on a baking sheet and place under the broiler until the cheese is lightly browned.

Nutritional Analyses (per serving, not including soup croutons)

	BEFORE	AFTER		BEFORE	AFTER
Calories	350	214	Cholesterol	50 mg	12 mg
Protein	13 g	12 g	Fiber	4 g	4 g
Carbohydrates	24 g	23 g	Sodium	750 mg	381 mg
Fat	22 g	7 g	% Calories from Fat	56	31
Saturated Fat	14 g	3.3 g	Omega-3 Fatty Acids	.3 g	.04 g
Monounsaturated Fat	5 g	2.2 g	Omega-6 Fatty Acids	.8 g	.4 g
Polyunsaturated Fat	2 g	.4 g			

Soup Croutons

Makes 5 servings

6 slices sourdough or French bread, sliced on the diagonal

Olive oil cooking spray or canola oil cooking spray

2 tablespoons [10 g] shredded or grated Parmesan cheese

1. Preheat the oven to 325°F [170°C].

2. Coat both sides of the bread with the cooking spray. Place the bread on a cookie sheet and sprinkle with the Parmesan (about 1 teaspoon [6 g] per slice).

3. Bake until crisp and golden brown, about 15 minutes.

Nutritional Analyses (per serving)

	BEFORE	AFTER		BEFORE	AFTER
Calories	219	185	Cholesterol	12 mg	1 mg
Protein	7 g	6.5 g	Fiber	2 g	2 g
Carbohydrates	33 g	33 g	Sodium	471 mg	418 mg
Fat	6.5 g	2.5 g	% Calories from Fat	26	12
Saturated Fat	3.2 g	.8 g	Omega-3 Fatty Acids	.08 g	.03 g
Monounsaturated Fat	2.1 g	1.2 g	Omega-6 Fatty Acids	.5 g	.4 g
Polyunsaturated Fat	.6 g	.5 g			

Chicken Pot Pie Soup

Makes 6 servings

If you crave homey foods like chicken pot pie and hearty soup, this is the dish for you!

4 cups [720 g] peeled and cubed potatoes

3 cups [720 g] low-sodium chicken broth

1 cup [120 g] chopped celery

1 cup [160 g] chopped onions

2 tablespoons [8 g] finely chopped fresh parsley (or 1½ teaspoons [1 g] dried parsley)

⅛ teaspoon [dash] freshly ground black pepper

1 tablespoon [8 g] unbleached white flour

1½ cups [363 g] fat-free half-and-half (or low-fat milk)

½ cup [73 g] petite peas (frozen peas work well)

2 cups [280 g] shredded or diced skinless and boneless roasted chicken breast

1 cup [113 g] shredded reduced-fat sharp Cheddar cheese

Salt to taste

1. Place the potatoes, chicken broth, celery, onions, parsley, and pepper in a large saucepan. Bring to a gentle boil, reduce the heat, and cover the pan. Simmer until tender (about 10 minutes).

2. Combine the flour with 2 tablespoons of the half-and-half and whisk. Whisk in the remaining half-and-half.

3. Add the half-and-half mixture and the green peas to the soup mixture; stir well. Cover the saucepan and simmer until the soup thickens (about 8 to 10 minutes).

4. Stir in the chicken and Cheddar and simmer to melt the cheese. Salt to taste and serve.

Nutritional Analyses (per serving)

	BEFORE	AFTER		BEFORE	AFTER
Calories	524	319	Cholesterol	95 mg	58 mg
Protein	23.5 g	29.3 g	Fiber	4.4 g	4.4 g
Carbohydrates	29 g	35 g	Sodium	284 mg	366 mg
Fat	34 g	6.8 g	% Calories from Fat	59	19
Saturated Fat	12.2 g	3.6 g	Omega-3 Fatty Acids	.3 g	.1 g
Monounsaturated Fat	10 g	.7 g	Omega-6 Fatty Acids	9.5 g	.4 g
Polyunsaturated Fat	10 g	.4 g			

Chicken and Sausage Gumbo

Makes 4 large servings

I've turned this gumbo around nutritionally by using brown rice, diced skinless chicken breast, and instead of hot-sausage links, I used a ⅔-less-fat turkey polska kielbasa sausage. Because a lot of the spice in the original recipe came from the hot links, I added some Creole seasoning to the mix.

2 cups [480 g] low-sodium chicken broth

2 cups [390 g] cooked brown rice (about ¾ cup [143 g] dry)

2 cups [500 g] tomato sauce (low-sodium, if available)

2 cups [280 g] diced roasted or cooked skinless chicken breast

1 (14½-ounce [411-g]) can diced, peeled tomatoes with liquid (Italian herb variety, if available)

8 ounces [227 g] ⅔-less-fat turkey polska kielbasa sausage, skin removed, and links cut in half lengthwise and then sliced

1 cup [164 g] frozen corn

1 cup [284 g] frozen cut okra

1 green bell pepper, finely diced, stem and seeds discarded

1 teaspoon [2 g] Creole seasoning (or more to taste)

1. Bring chicken broth and 2 cups [474 g] water to a boil in a large saucepan.

2. Add the remaining ingredients to the saucepan and stir to blend well. Cover the saucepan and continue to cook over medium heat for 15 to 20 minutes, or until heated through. Serve hot.

Nutritional Analyses (per serving)

	BEFORE	AFTER		BEFORE	AFTER
Calories	621	445	Cholesterol	81 mg	82 mg
Protein	28 g	38 g	Fiber	8 g	7.2 g
Carbohydrates	35 g	60 g	Sodium	4,604 mg	1,000 mg
Fat	41 g	6.5 g	% Calories from Fat	60	13
Saturated Fat	11 g	1.9 g	Omega-3 Fatty Acids	.5 g	.1 g
Monounsaturated Fat	16 g	1.4 g	Omega-6 Fatty Acids	11.6 g	1.1 g
Polyunsaturated Fat	12 g	1.2 g			

Cabernet and Hoisin Beef Stew

Makes 8 servings

Beef stew is one of the top comfort foods. This elegant variation on the traditional version is equally comforting. Since there is quite a bit of chopped onion in this recipe, you can save some time and tears by using a food processor (in two batches, depending on the size of your food processor) or hand chopper to chop the onions. You can make this stew a day ahead. Just cool it slightly and chill uncovered in the refrigerator until cold, then you can cover it. To serve the next day, bring the stew to a simmer on the stove, stirring often. You can serve it over cooked egg noodles, if desired.

2 tablespoons [28 g] olive oil, divided

2½ pounds [1.13 kg] boneless beef chuck roast, trimmed of all visible fat and cut into 2½-inch [63-mm] pieces

½ teaspoon [3 g] freshly ground black pepper

3 cups [480 g] chopped onions

2 cups [472 g] cabernet sauvignon, divided

1 (14½-ounce [411-g]) can Italian-style diced tomatoes with liquid

½ cup [128 g] bottled hoisin sauce (available in the Asian-food section of most supermarkets)

2 bay leaves

1 pound [454 g] slender whole carrots, cut diagonally into 1-inch lengths (about 2 cups [256 g])

1 tablespoon [8 g] cornstarch mixed with 1 tablespoon [14 g] water

Salt and black pepper to taste

2 tablespoons [8 g] chopped fresh parsley

1. Heat 1 tablespoon [14 g] of the olive oil in an extra-large nonstick skillet over high heat. Sprinkle the meat with a little bit of pepper. Add the meat pieces to the skillet and sauté until nicely brown on all sides (about 8 minutes).

2. Meanwhile, add the remaining oil to the center of a large nonstick saucepan. Add the onions and sauté until golden brown (about 4 to 6 minutes). Mix the meat into the onions. Add 1 cup [236 g] of the wine, the tomatoes with liquid, hoisin sauce, and bay leaves. Bring to a boil.

3. Reduce the heat to low, cover the pot, and simmer for 45 minutes, stirring occasionally. Add the carrots and the remaining wine. Cover the pan and simmer for 30 minutes longer, stirring occasionally.

4. Uncover the saucepan and increase the heat to high. Boil until the sauce is slightly thickened, stirring occasionally (about 15 minutes longer). Reduce the heat to medium, add the cornstarch mixture, and simmer until the sauce thickens, stirring occasionally (about 5 minutes). Discard the bay leaves. Season the stew with salt and pepper to taste. Ladle the stew into individual bowls and sprinkle each serving with fresh parsley. You can also serve each serving of stew over a small serving of cooked egg noodles.

Nutritional Analyses (per serving)

	BEFORE	AFTER		BEFORE	AFTER
Calories	615	452	Cholesterol	136 mg	113 mg
Protein	32 g	36 g	Fiber	4 g	4 g
Carbohydrates	28 g	28 g	Sodium	567 mg	558 mg
Fat	37 g	16 g	% Calories from Fat	54	32
Saturated Fat	12 g	5.5 g	Omega-3 Fatty Acids	.4 g	.1 g
Monounsaturated Fat	19 g	8.3 g	Omega-6 Fatty Acids	2 g	1.1 g
Polyunsaturated Fat	2.4 g	1.2 g			

Light Newport Clam Chowder

Makes 6 servings

The original Newport clam chowder recipe won the chowder cook-off in Rhode Island a few years ago. But considering how fat-filled that version was, I figured I should perform a recipe makeover before sampling it. For the lightened version, the butter was cut in half and some wine or chicken broth and celery were added for flavor.

2 tablespoons [28 g] butter

1½ cups [180 g] sliced celery

1 cup [160 g] chopped onions

⅓ cup [41 g] all-purpose flour

⅓ cup [81 g] low-fat milk

⅓ cup [79 g] white wine, nonalcoholic or
   light beer, or low-sodium chicken broth

2 (8-ounce [236-ml]) jars clam juice

2 (5-ounce [142-g]) cans boiled baby clams
   in juice (do not drain)

4 medium red or white potatoes, peeled and
   cut into ½-inch [13-mm] cubes

1½ cups [363 g] fat-free half-and-half

Salt and black pepper to taste

½ teaspoon [1 g] chopped fresh dill weed

½ cup [57 g] shredded reduced-fat sharp
   Cheddar cheese (optional)

1. Melt the butter in a large nonstick saucepan or stockpot over medium heat. Add the celery and onions and sauté until the onions are transparent (about 3 to 5 minutes).

2. Using a whisk, blend the flour and milk in a small bowl. Whisk in the wine. Turn off the heat and stir while adding the mixture to the onions and celery.

3. In a separate pot, bring the clam juice and clams to a boil. Reduce the heat and simmer, uncovered, for 15 minutes.

4. In a medium saucepan, cover the potatoes with water. Bring to a boil and cook until the potatoes are tender (about 10 minutes). Drain and set aside. (You can microwave them until tender if you prefer.)

5. Slowly pour the hot clam stock into the butter-flour mixture, stirring constantly. Continue stirring and slowly bring to a boil. Reduce the heat and add the cooked potatoes. Mix in the half-and-half, salt and pepper to taste, and the dill weed. Heat through, but do not boil.

6. Sprinkle each serving with Cheddar (if desired) and serve.

Nutritional Analyses (per serving)

	BEFORE	AFTER		BEFORE	AFTER
Calories	375	310	Cholesterol	101 mg	54 mg
Protein	14 g	17 g	Fiber	4.5 g	4 g
Carbohydrates	40 g	48 g	Sodium	543 mg	538 mg
Fat	18 g	6 g	% Calories from Fat	43	17
Saturated Fat	11 g	3 g	Omega-3 Fatty Acids	.1 g	.1 g
Monounsaturated Fat	5 g	1.2 g	Omega-6 Fatty Acids	.2 g	.1 g
Polyunsaturated Fat	.4 g	.2 g			

Hearty Beef and Vegetable Stew

Makes 8 servings

An extra-lean round tip steak is used in this recipe to provide the beef cubes for the stew, and I've cranked up the vegetables a bit to boost nutrients and fiber. The only cooking fat added is a tablespoon of canola oil to brown the meat on the outside.

2 pounds [.9 kg] round tip beef, trimmed of any visible fat and cut into 1-inch [25-mm] cubes

½ teaspoon [3 g] salt (optional)

½ teaspoon [3 g] black pepper

1 tablespoon [14 g] canola oil

2 cups [320 g] chopped onions

Canola oil cooking spray

1 tablespoon [9 g] minced or chopped garlic

3 tablespoons [23 g] unbleached flour

1 cup [236 g] merlot (or similar red wine)

2 cups [480 g] low-sodium beef broth

2 bay leaves

1 teaspoon [1 g] dried thyme

3 cups [384 g] baby carrots

1 cup [144 g] frozen peas

3 tablespoons [11 g] chopped fresh parsley leaves

1. Preheat the oven to 200°F [93°C]. Place the meat in a large bowl. Sprinkle with salt (if desired) and pepper; toss to coat.

2. Heat the oil in a large nonstick saucepan (ovenproof) over medium-high heat; add the meat and brown on all sides (about 5 minutes). Transfer the meat temporarily to a bowl.

3. Add the onions to the saucepan and sauté until almost softened (about 4 minutes), adding the cooking spray as needed. Reduce the heat to medium and stir in the garlic; sauté for 30 seconds longer.

4. Add the flour to a 2-cup [.5 l] measuring cup and stir in ¼ cup [59 g] of the wine until smooth. Stir in the remaining wine. Add this mixture to the saucepan with the onions and stir in the beef broth, bay leaves, and thyme; bring to a simmer. Add the beef and baby carrots to the stew and return to a simmer. Cover the saucepan and place it in the oven. Cook the stew for about 2½ hours (until the beef is tender).

5. Stir in the peas and parsley, cover the saucepan, and let it stand for 5 minutes to blend the flavors. Serve with a slice of crusty bread.

Nutritional Analyses (per serving)

	BEFORE	AFTER		BEFORE	AFTER
Calories	518	280	Cholesterol	110 mg	70 mg
Protein	34 g	27 g	Fiber	3 g	4 g
Carbohydrates	17 g	17 g	Sodium	300 mg	121 mg
Fat	32 g	9 g	% Calories from Fat	56	29
Saturated Fat	11 g	2.8 g	Omega-3 Fatty Acids	.4 g	.2 g
Monounsaturated Fat	13 g	3.8 g	Omega-6 Fatty Acids	3.8 g	.7 g
Polyunsaturated Fat	4.2 g	.9 g			

Homemade Lentil Soup

Makes 8 large soup servings

If you're trying to eat more beans (and all of us should, because they are high in fiber and phytochemicals), lentil soup is a good place to start. Because of their tiny size, lentils can cook in about 30 minutes. The original recipe I lightened called for ½ cup [108 g] bacon fat. Here I've used a couple of tablespoons of olive oil instead.

2 tablespoons [28 g] olive oil
2 cups [320 g] chopped onions
4 teaspoons [11 g] minced or crushed garlic
8 cups [2 kg] low-sodium chicken broth
1 pound [454 g] dried lentils, washed and
   picked over
4 Roma tomatoes, quartered

2 potatoes, washed and diced
2 large carrots, diced
2 tablespoons [6 g] finely chopped fresh
   oregano leaves (or 1½ teaspoons [3 g]
   dried oregano)
¾ teaspoon [2 g] freshly ground black pepper
Salt and black pepper to taste

1. Heat the olive oil in a large saucepan and sauté the onions and garlic until lightly browned.

2. Add the other ingredients and bring to a boil. Cover and let the soup boil for 15 minutes.

3. Lower the heat and simmer for approximately 30 to 60 minutes.

Nutritional Analyses (per serving)

	BEFORE	AFTER		BEFORE	AFTER
Calories	445	344	Cholesterol	14 mg	4 mg
Protein	22 g	20 g	Fiber	16 g	16 g
Carbohydrates	55 g	55.5 g	Sodium	870 mg	125 mg
Fat	16 g	5.5 g	% Calories from Fat	33	14
Saturated Fat	7 g	1.4 g	Omega-3 Fatty Acids	.3 g	.1 g
Monounsaturated Fat	6.6 g	2.8 g	Omega-6 Fatty Acids	1.5 g	.6 g
Polyunsaturated Fat	1.7 g	.7 g			

CHAPTER FIVE

Small but Mighty Side Dishes

Believe it or not, some of us consider side dishes to be the most comforting of all. You know, we're talking about that green bean casserole served on holidays or corn casserole or those greens that remind you of Grandma's Sunday suppers. A variety of recipes are presented here in lightened versions, but they are still super side dishes that are supercomforting.

Mashed Potatoes and Savory Gravy

Makes 6 servings

I purposely don't add butter to this mashed potato recipe so I can include a pat at the table.

2 pounds [907 g] russet, Yukon gold, or white potatoes, peeled and cut into chunks

1 teaspoon [6 g] salt, plus more to taste

1 cup [242 g] low-fat milk, fat-free half-and-half, or a mixture of the two

¼ cup [61 g] fat-free or light sour cream

¼ teaspoon [1 g] freshly ground black pepper

¼ teaspoon [1 g] freshly grated nutmeg (optional)

3 tablespoons butter [42 g], 1 teaspoon [5 g] to top each serving (optional)

1. Place the potatoes in a large microwave-safe dish. Cover the dish with cold water, sprinkle with salt, and toss together. Cover and microwave on high for 10 minutes. Gently stir the mixture, cover, and microwave on high for another 10 minutes, or until the potatoes are very tender. Drain the potatoes and transfer to the bowl of an electric mixer.

2. Add the milk and/or half-and-half to a 2-cup [.5 l] glass measuring cup and heat in the microwave on high until very hot (1 to 2 minutes).

3. Meanwhile, beat the potatoes in the mixer on low speed until the lumps have disappeared (about 1 minute). Add the sour cream and mix on low speed, pouring in the hot milk slowly. Add the pepper and nutmeg, if desired, and mix. Serve with a daub of butter and Savory Gravy (recipe follows).

Nutritional Analyses (the "after" figures are per serving, not including optional butter garnish)

	BEFORE	AFTER		BEFORE	AFTER
Calories	235	151	Cholesterol	30 mg	3 mg
Protein	4 g	5 g	Fiber	2 g	2 g
Carbohydrates	31 g	32 g	Sodium	319 mg	246 mg
Fat	11 g	.7 g	% Calories from Fat	42	4
Saturated Fat	7 g	.4 g	Omega-3 Fatty Acids	.2 g	.01 g
Monounsaturated Fat	3 g	.1 g	Omega-6 Fatty Acids	.3 g	.04 g
Polyunsaturated Fat	.5 g	.1 g			

Savory Gravy

Makes at least 2 cups [466 g] of gravy (8 servings with ¼ cup [58 g] gravy per serving)

2 tablespoons [28 g] chicken, turkey, beef, or pork drippings (or 2 tablespoons [58 g] canola oil)

1 cup [251 g] condensed chicken or beef broth (or 1 cup [237 g] hot water mixed with 2 to 3 teaspoons [12 to 18 g] bouillon)

4 tablespoons [31 g] Wondra quick-mixing flour

1 cup [242 g] low-fat milk, whole milk, or fat-free half-and-half (or a mixture of ½ cup [121 g] fat-free half-and-half and ½ cup [121 g] low-fat milk)

¼ teaspoon [1 g] poultry seasoning (optional)

½ cup [73 g] finely chopped cooked chicken or turkey breast (optional)

Salt and black pepper to taste

1. Add the drippings, 2 tablespoons [12 g] of the condensed broth, and flour to a large glass measuring cup and whisk until blended. Whisk in the remaining broth and the milk.

2. Microwave on high for 5 minutes. Stir and microwave on high for another 5 minutes, or until nicely thickened.

3. Stir in the poultry seasoning (if desired), chicken, and salt and pepper to taste. Serve hot. You can keep the dish covered in the refrigerator and reheat as needed.

Nutritional Analyses (per serving)

	BEFORE	AFTER		BEFORE	AFTER
Calories	120	65	Cholesterol	22 mg	5 mg
Protein	3 g	3 g	Fiber	.1 g	.1 g
Carbohydrates	4 g	5 g	Sodium	211 mg	212 mg
Fat	10 g	3.8 g	% Calories from Fat	73	52
Saturated Fat	4 g	1.2 g	Omega-3 Fatty Acids	.1 g	.05 g
Monounsaturated Fat	4 g	1.6 g	Omega-6 Fatty Acids	1.4 g	.7 g
Polyunsaturated Fat	2 g	.8 g			

Curried Cauliflower

Makes 8 servings

This creamy cauliflower casserole is a comforting side dish that's good for you, too!

Canola oil cooking spray

1 large head of cauliflower, broken into small florets (about 8 cups [800 g])

1 (10¾-ounce [318-ml]) can reduced-fat condensed cream of chicken soup

½ cup [121 g] fat-free sour cream

¼ cup [58 g] light mayonnaise

¼ cup [61 g] low-fat milk or fat-free half-and-half

1½ teaspoons [3 g] curry powder

½ cup [54 g] reduced-fat wheat crackers, crushed (you can crush crackers using a small food processor)

1 tablespoon [14 g] melted butter or no-trans margarine

1. Preheat the oven to 350°F [180°C]. Coat a 2-quart [2 l] baking dish with the cooking spray.

2. Place the cauliflower pieces in a large microwave-safe dish with ½ cup [119 g] of water. Cover and microwave on high until just tender but still firm (about 8 minutes). Drain the cauliflower well and add it to the prepared baking dish.

3. In a medium-sized bowl, whisk together the soup, sour cream, mayonnaise, milk, and curry powder until well blended. Pour the mixture over the cauliflower.

4. In a bowl, blend the crackers with the butter and sprinkle it over the cauliflower mixture.

5. Bake, uncovered, for 30 minutes. Serve hot.

Nutritional Analyses (per serving)

	BEFORE	AFTER		BEFORE	AFTER
Calories	280	119	Cholesterol	30 mg	11 mg
Protein	4 g	5 g	Fiber	3 g	3 g
Carbohydrates	11 g	15 g	Sodium	532 mg	289 mg
Fat	26 g	5 g	% Calories from Fat	83	38
Saturated Fat	7 g	1.8 g	Omega-3 Fatty Acids	.2 g	.1 g
Monounsaturated Fat	8 g	.4 g	Omega-6 Fatty Acids	7 g	.06 g
Polyunsaturated Fat	10 g	.2 g			

Popular Picnic Broccoli Salad

Makes 8 side servings

I've seen this broccoli salad served at countless barbecues and church functions, and I was shocked by the amount of mayonnaise it used. No one wants to spend all their calories and fat on just one side dish! I cut the mayonnaise down to ¼ cup [56 g] and added ¾ cup [182 g] of fat-free sour cream (you can make this with ⅛ cup [27 g] of mayonnaise and 14 tablespoons [212 g] of fat-free sour cream, too).

6 slices turkey bacon

6 cups [840 g] bite-size broccoli pieces (about 2 heads)

½ cup [73 g] raisins

¼ cup [40 g] finely chopped red onion (add more, if desired)

2 tablespoons [25 g] granulated sugar

3 tablespoons [45 g] white wine vinegar

¼ cup [58 g] mayonnaise

¾ cup [182 g] fat-free sour cream

½ cup [64 g] roasted sunflower seeds (lightly salted)

1. Place the bacon in a large nonstick skillet and cook over medium heat, flipping it often, until brown and crispy. Cool, then crumble it into little bits and set aside.

2. In a large salad bowl, toss the broccoli pieces together with the raisins and red onion.

3. In a large measuring cup, whisk together the sugar, vinegar, mayonnaise, and sour cream. Pour over the broccoli mixture and toss to coat well.

4. Refrigerate for at least 2 hours to allow the flavors to blend. Before serving, sprinkle the sunflower seeds and crumbled bacon over the top, toss, and serve.

Nutritional Analyses (per serving)

	BEFORE	AFTER		BEFORE	AFTER
Calories	401	209	Cholesterol	23 mg	13 mg
Protein	10 g	7 g	Fiber	3.3 g	3.5 g
Carbohydrates	20 g	22 g	Sodium	303 mg	213 mg
Fat	31 g	11.8 g	% Calories from Fat	70	48
Saturated Fat	5.5 g	1.8 g	Omega-3 Fatty Acids	1 g	2 g
Monounsaturated Fat	9.3 g	3 g	Omega-6 Fatty Acids	15 g	4 g
Polyunsaturated Fat	16 g	6.1 g			

Potatoes with Leeks and Gruyère

Makes 12 servings

This is a super dish for Easter dinner or any other special occasion—it can even be baked the day before. Just cook it, cover it, and pop it into the refrigerator. When you're ready to eat, cook it, uncovered, in a 350°F [180°C] oven for about 20 minutes.

Canola oil cooking spray

1 tablespoon [14 g] olive or canola oil

1 pound leeks [454 g] (white and pale green parts only), thinly sliced

1 (8-ounce [227-g]) package light cream cheese, at room temperature

1 teaspoon [6 g] salt

1 teaspoon [6 g] freshly ground black pepper

¼ teaspoon [1 g] ground nutmeg (more if desired)

1 cup [242 g] fat-free half-and-half or low-fat milk

1 large egg

½ cup [126 g] egg substitute

2 pounds [907 g] frozen hash browns, shredded and thawed somewhat

2 cups [216 g] grated Gruyère cheese

1 teaspoon [.5 g] dried parsley, or Italian herb blend, or fines herbs (optional)

1. Preheat the oven to 350°F [180°C]. Coat a 13 x 9 x 2-inch [22 x 23 x 5-cm] baking dish with the cooking spray.

2. Add the oil to a large nonstick skillet over medium heat. Add the leeks and sauté until tender (about 8 minutes). Remove from the heat and set aside.

3. Combine the cream cheese, salt, pepper, and nutmeg in the bowl of an electric mixer and beat on low until blended. Slowly pour in the half-and-half, egg, and egg substitute, one at a time, and beat just until blended.

4. Stir the leeks, hash browns, and Gruyère into the milk mixture and pour into the prepared baking dish. Sprinkle the parsley over the top, if desired.

5. Bake until the mixture is cooked throughout and the top is brown (about 55 to 60 minutes). Cool slightly and serve.

Nutritional Analyses (per serving)

	BEFORE	AFTER		BEFORE	AFTER
Calories	334	237	Cholesterol	126 mg	47 mg
Protein	11 g	13 g	Fiber	2.5 g	2.5 g
Carbohydrates	21 g	24 g	Sodium	430 mg	422 mg
Fat	24 g	10 g	% Calories from Fat	64	38
Saturated Fat	14 g	5.8 g	Omega-3 Fatty Acids	.3 g	.1 g
Monounsaturated Fat	7.1 g	2.9 g	Omega-6 Fatty Acids	.8 g	.4 g
Polyunsaturated Fat	1.1 g	.5 g			

Grandma's Collard Greens

Makes 6 servings (1 cup [36 g] of cooked greens per serving)

The key ingredients in many "greens" recipes, aside from the greens themselves, are ham hocks and salt pork. In this lighter version, I keep the ham and salt pork flavor with extra-lean finely diced ham and some low-sodium beef or chicken broth.

1 cup (about 5 ounces [142 g]) extra-lean diced ham

1 quart [960 g] low-sodium beef or chicken broth

1 cup [160 g] finely chopped onions

2 bay leaves

2 tablespoons [40 g] maple syrup (reduced-calorie pancake syrup can be substituted)

¼ teaspoon [2 g] red pepper flakes (add more, if desired)

16 cups [216 g] collard greens, packed, rinsed, stemmed, and thinly sliced (about 3 bunches of greens)

2 teaspoons [10 g] red wine vinegar

Freshly ground black pepper to taste

Salt to taste (optional)

1. Place the ham, broth, onions, bay leaves, maple syrup, and red pepper flakes in a large saucepan and stir to blend. Bring to a boil over high heat, then reduce to simmer. Cook, uncovered, for 15 minutes.

2. Stir in the collard greens and bring back to a boil over high heat. Reduce the heat to simmer and cook the greens, uncovered, until tender (about 30 minutes). Sprinkle the vinegar over the top and add pepper to taste (salt, too, if desired).

Nutritional Analyses (per serving)

	BEFORE	AFTER		BEFORE	AFTER
Calories	461	125	Cholesterol	86 mg	5 mg
Protein	21 g	12 g	Fiber	4.8 g	4.8 g
Carbohydrates	13 g	14 g	Sodium	478 mg	295 mg
Fat	36 g	2.8 g	% Calories from Fat	70	22
Saturated Fat	14 g	.8 g	Omega-3 Fatty Acids	.4 g	.2 g
Monounsaturated Fat	16 g	1.1 g	Omega-6 Fatty Acids	3.8 g	.5 g
Polyunsaturated Fat	4.2 g	.7 g			

Day-Before Mashed Potatoes

Makes 8 servings

This recipe makes a thick mashed potato that stands up well after a night in the refrigerator.

8 medium-sized potatoes, peeled and cubed

1 tablespoon [14 g] butter or
   no- or low-trans margarine

⅔ cup [159 g] light cream cheese

⅔ cup [160 g] fat-free or light sour cream

2 teaspoons [12 g] onion powder

1 teaspoon [6 g] salt (optional)

¼ teaspoon [1 g] ground black pepper

Canola oil cooking spray

1 to 2 tablespoons [14 to 28 g]
   butter (optional)

1. Preheat the oven to 350°F [180°C]. Bring a large pot of salted water to a boil. Drop in the potatoes and cook until tender (about 15 minutes).

2. Drain the potatoes well and immediately add them to the bowl of an electric mixer along with the tablespoon of butter. Beat on low until the potatoes are smooth.

3. Mix in the cream cheese, sour cream, onion powder, salt (if desired), and pepper and beat on low to blend well. Adjust the seasoning to taste.

4. Coat a 9 x 13-inch [23 x 33-cm] baking dish with the cooking spray. Spread the potato mixture in the prepared dish and refrigerate overnight.

5. Bake for 30 minutes. Dot each serving with a little bit of butter, if desired.

Nutritional Analyses (per serving)

	BEFORE	AFTER		BEFORE	AFTER
Calories	350	240	Cholesterol	45 mg	17 mg
Protein	6 g	7 g	Fiber	4 g	4 g
Carbohydrates	45 g	47 g	Sodium	430 mg	117 mg
Fat	17 g	3.5 g	% Calories from Fat	43	13
Saturated Fat	10.5 g	2.1 g	Omega-3 Fatty Acids	.2 g	.05 g
Monounsaturated Fat	4.7 g	.4 g	Omega-6 Fatty Acids	4 g	.1 g
Polyunsaturated Fat	.7 g	.2 g			

Savory Corn Casserole

Makes 8 servings

If you like corn, you'll like this side dish. The original recipe called for quite a bit of mayonnaise, cream of mushroom soup, Cheddar cheese, eggs, and 8 tablespoons [112 g] of butter (if you can believe it!). I used a tablespoon of butter, reduced-fat cheese and Ritz crackers, much less mayonnaise, and added some fat-free sour cream, low-fat milk, and egg substitute.

Canola oil cooking spray

1 tablespoon [14 g] butter or no- or low-trans margarine

1 (16-ounce [454-g]) bag frozen corn

⅔ cup [188 g] reduced-fat condensed cream of mushroom soup

½ cup [57 g] grated reduced-fat sharp Cheddar cheese

½ cup [121 g] low-fat milk or fat-free half-and-half

¼ cup [63 g] egg substitute (2 egg whites can be substituted)

⅓ cup [33 g] chopped green onions

6 tablespoons [91 g] fat-free sour cream

2 tablespoons [28 g] light mayonnaise

1 large egg

20 reduced-fat Ritz (or similar) crackers, crumbled

A pinch or two of paprika (optional)

1. Preheat the oven to 350°F [180°C]. Coat a 9 x 9-inch [23 x 23-cm] baking dish with the cooking spray.

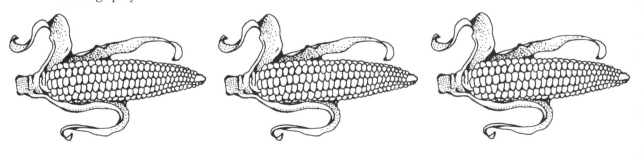

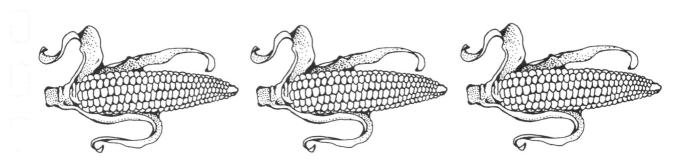

2. Melt the butter in a medium-sized microwave-safe bowl on high for about 30 seconds. Stir in the remaining ingredients, except the crackers and paprika. Spread the mixture evenly in the prepared dish.

3. Sprinkle the crackers over the casserole and add a pinch or two of paprika, if desired. Bake until the casserole is bubbly and lightly browned around the sides (about 50 minutes). When it comes out of the oven, the middle may not be completely set, but in about 5 to 7 minutes after being out of the oven it should be ready to serve.

Nutritional Analyses (per serving)

	BEFORE	AFTER		BEFORE	AFTER
Calories	335	165	Cholesterol	95 mg	40 mg
Protein	7 g	7 g	Fiber	1.8 g	1.8 g
Carbohydrates	22 g	20 g	Sodium	666 mg	267 mg
Fat	25 g	6.4 g	% Calories from Fat	67	35
Saturated Fat	11 g	2.9 g	Omega-3 Fatty Acids	.2 g	.03 g
Monounsaturated Fat	4.5 g	.8 g	Omega-6 Fatty Acids	.2 g	.3g
Polyunsaturated Fat	2.4 g	.4 g			

Creamy Spinach Casserole

Makes 9 servings

Even if you aren't crazy about spinach, you might enjoy this dish for the cream cheese, crunchy water chestnuts, and savory turkey bacon bits.

1 (14-ounce [397-g]) can artichoke hearts (in water), drained and chopped (2 cups [336 g])

2 (10-ounce [283-g]) boxes frozen spinach, chopped

1 cup [124 g] water chestnuts, sliced (a jicama, peeled and chopped, can be substituted)

6 ounces [170 g] light cream cheese

2 tablespoons [30 g] fat-free half-and-half or low-fat milk

½ cup [15 g] fat-free or low-fat herb-seasoned croutons

4 slices turkey bacon, cooked crisp and crumbled (optional)

1. Preheat the oven to 350°F [180°C]. Spread the artichoke hearts on the bottom of a 9 x 9-inch [23 x 23-cm] baking dish.

2. Cook the spinach according to the package directions, drain well, and place in the bowl of an electric mixer. While the spinach is still hot, add the water chestnuts, cream cheese, and half-and-half and beat on low speed. Pour the mixture over the artichoke hearts.

3. Blend the croutons and bacon bits (if desired) and sprinkle them over the top of the casserole. Bake for about 30 minutes. Serve hot.

Nutritional Analyses (per serving)

	BEFORE	AFTER		BEFORE	AFTER
Calories	192	112	Cholesterol	27 mg	15 mg
Protein	7.5 g	6.5 g	Fiber	3.5 g	3.5 g
Carbohydrates	13 g	12 g	Sodium	485 mg	540 mg
Fat	13 g	4.3 g	% Calories from Fat	61	35
Saturated Fat	5.4 g	2.5 g	Omega-3 Fatty Acids	.1 g	.01 g
Monounsaturated Fat	3.8 g	.5 g	Omega-6 Fatty Acids	.4 g	.3g
Polyunsaturated Fat	.6 g	.3 g			

Green Bean Casserole

Makes 8 servings

For many families it wouldn't be a holiday dinner without a green bean casserole. I made a few ingredient changes to transform this dish into a lighter version of its former self. Don't worry; you'll still be able to recognize it!

2 (10-ounce [283-g]) boxes French-style
frozen green beans
1 (10¾-ounce [318-ml]) can condensed
cream of mushroom soup
¼ cup [61 g] fat-free sour cream
¼ cup [61 g] fat-free half-and-half
(or low-fat milk)

1 teaspoon [16 g] light soy sauce
Dash of freshly ground black pepper
1 tablespoon [9 g] diced pimiento (optional)
¼ cup [35 g] almonds, sliced or slivered and
toasted until lightly browned

1. Preheat the oven to 350°F [180°C]. Cook the green beans according to the package instructions; drain well.

2. In a 1-quart [1 l] casserole dish or 9-inch square [23 x 23-cm] baking dish, combine the soup, sour cream, half-and-half, soy sauce, pepper, and pimiento (if desired). Stir in the green beans.

3. Bake for 20 minutes, or until bubbly. Sprinkle the almonds over the top and bake for 5 minutes longer.

Nutritional Analyses (per serving)

	BEFORE	AFTER		BEFORE	AFTER
Calories	100	68	Cholesterol	10 mg	2 mg
Protein	3.5 g	3.5 g	Fiber	2.4 g	2.4 g
Carbohydrates	9 g	9.2 g	Sodium	189 mg	47 mg
Fat	6 g	2.5 g	% Calories from Fat	55	32
Saturated Fat	2.5 g	.4 g	Omega-3 Fatty Acids	.1 g	.1 g
Monounsaturated Fat	2.1 g	1.1 g	Omega-6 Fatty Acids	1.1 g	.7g
Polyunsaturated Fat	1.2 g	.8 g			

Marshmallow Whipped Sweet Potatoes

Makes 6 servings

We all know and love this holiday dinner favorite. To make sure it's not a holiday diet-buster, I've reduced the amount of butter used and added some orange juice in its place. I've reduced the amount of marshmallows a tad, too. If you want to make enough for a dinner party (say twelve people), you can double all the ingredients and use a 3- to 4-quart [3 to 4 l] baking dish.

Canola oil cooking spray
3 cups [480 g] hot sweet potatoes or yams, mashed
3 tablespoons [47 g] orange juice

1 tablespoon [14 g] butter or no-trans margarine
¼ teaspoon [1 g] salt
1½ cups [75 g] miniature marshmallows

1. Preheat the oven to 350°F [180°C]. Coat a 1½-quart [1.5-l] baking dish with the cooking spray.

2. Combine the sweet potatoes, orange juice, butter, and salt in the bowl of an electric mixer. Add 1 cup [50 g] of the marshmallows and beat on medium speed until fluffy. If the marshmallows aren't melting, microwave the bowl for a minute and resume beating.

3. Spoon the mixture into the prepared baking dish. Sprinkle the remaining marshmallows over the top and bake for about 15 minutes. The marshmallows on top should be lightly browned.

Nutritional Analyses (per serving)

	BEFORE	AFTER		BEFORE	AFTER
Calories	225	191	Cholesterol	20 mg	5 mg
Protein	3 g	3 g	Fiber	4 g	4 g
Carbohydrates	45 g	42 g	Sodium	195 mg	135 mg
Fat	8 g	2 g	% Calories from Fat	27	10
Saturated Fat	5 g	1.2 g	Omega-3 Fatty Acids	.1 g	.1 g
Monounsaturated Fat	2.2 g	.6 g	Omega-6 Fatty Acids	.2 g	.1g
Polyunsaturated Fat	.4 g	.2 g			

Light Potato Salad

Makes 8 servings (¾ cup [188 g] each)

I like this recipe because it's a "back to basics" type of potato salad. If you want to give this dish a little kick, add extra sweet-pickle relish, onion, celery, pimientos, and sun-dried tomatoes or kalamata olives.

2 pounds [907 g] russet potatoes, peeled and diced

¾ cup [182 g] fat-free sour cream

¼ cup [56 g] light mayonnaise

2 tablespoons [31 g] sweet-pickle relish

1 tablespoon [9 g] finely shredded or chopped carrot

1 tablespoon [9 g] finely minced celery

1 tablespoon [9 g] finely minced white onion

4 teaspoons [17 g] sugar

2 teaspoons [10 g] prepared mustard (add 1 more teaspoon [5 g], if desired)

1½ teaspoons [4 g] diced pimientos

1 teaspoon [5 g] vinegar

¼ teaspoon [1 g] black pepper

¼ teaspoon [1 g] dried parsley

Dash of salt (add more to taste)

1. Cook the potatoes in 6 cups [1,422 g] of salted, boiling water for 7 to 10 minutes. The potato chunks should be tender yet slightly tough in the middle when done. Drain and rinse in cold water.

2. In a medium-sized bowl, combine the remaining ingredients and whisk until smooth.

3. Transfer the drained potatoes to a large bowl and pour the dressing over them, gently tossing until well combined. Cover and chill for at least 4 hours (overnight is best).

Nutritional Analyses (per serving)

	BEFORE	AFTER		BEFORE	AFTER
Calories	320	166	Cholesterol	16 mg	5 mg
Protein	2.3 g	3 g	Fiber	1.8 g	1.8 g
Carbohydrates	28 g	32 g	Sodium	202 mg	129 mg
Fat	22 g	3 g	% Calories from Fat	62	16
Saturated Fat	4 g	.6 g	Omega-3 Fatty Acids	1 g	.3 g
Monounsaturated Fat	7 g	.5 g	Omega-6 Fatty Acids	7 g	1.2g
Polyunsaturated Fat	11 g	1.6 g			

Creamy au Gratin Potatoes

Makes 6 servings

The creamy cheese sauce and the tender potatoes in this classic French dish combine to make one of America's favorite comfort foods. I lightened this up quite a bit by using a lot less butter, switching to fat-free half-and-half (which holds up better than low-fat milk after being heated for an hour) and reduced-fat sharp Cheddar to give it a kick.

Canola oil cooking spray

3 tablespoons [15 g] shredded Parmesan cheese

3 tablespoons [11 g] fresh chopped parsley

3 large russet potatoes, peeled cut into ¼-inch [6-mm] slices

1 onion, sliced into thin rings

Salt and black pepper to taste

1½ tablespoons [21 g] butter

3 tablespoons [24 g] all-purpose flour

1½ cups [363 g] fat-free half-and-half or low-fat milk

1½ teaspoons [4 g] minced or chopped garlic

1½ cups [170 g] shredded reduced-fat sharp Cheddar cheese

1. Preheat the oven to 400°F [200°C]. Coat the entire inside of a 1- or 2-quart [1-or 2-l] baking dish with the cooking spray.

2. Combine the Parmesan and parsley in a small bowl and toss to blend.

3. Layer one-third of the potatoes in the bottom of the prepared casserole dish. Top with half of the onion slices and add salt and pepper to taste. Sprinkle 2 tablespoons [10 g] of the Parmesan and parsley mixture over the top.

4. Layer half of the remaining potatoes on top of the onion slices. Then add the remaining onion and salt and pepper to taste. Sprinkle 2 tablespoons [10 g] of the Parmesan and parsley mixture over the top. Layer the last of the potatoes on top of this.

5. In a medium-sized saucepan, melt the butter over medium heat and let it brown slightly; remove from the heat. In a small bowl, whisk together the flour and 4 tablespoons [60 g] of the half-and-half. Whisk in ¼ cup [61 g] more of the half-and-half and add the mixture to the butter. Continue to cook the mixture over medium heat, stirring constantly with a whisk, for 1 minute. Stir in the remaining half-and-half and the garlic. Cook until the mixture reaches the desired thickness (about 3 minutes). Stir in the Cheddar all at once, and continue stirring until it melts (about 30 to 60 seconds).

6. Pour the Cheddar sauce slowly over the potatoes and sprinkle the remaining Parmesan and parsley over the top. Cover the dish with aluminum foil (coat the side touching the potatoes with cooking spray so that it doesn't stick to the cheese sauce) and bake for 1 hour, or until the potatoes are tender. Serve hot.

Nutritional Analyses (per serving)

	BEFORE	AFTER		BEFORE	AFTER
Calories	468	334	Cholesterol	92 mg	32 mg
Protein	16 g	17 g	Fiber	4 g	4 g
Carbohydrates	39 g	45 g	Sodium	590 mg	590 mg
Fat	27 g	9.5 g	% Calories from Fat	52	26
Saturated Fat	17 g	6 g	Omega-3 Fatty Acids	.3 g	.1 g
Monounsaturated Fat	8 g	1.1 g	Omega-6 Fatty Acids	.5 g	.1g
Polyunsaturated Fat	1 g	.2 g			

Sage and Sausage Stuffing

Makes 6 servings

It isn't just the butter that did this original recipe in—it's the butter plus the sausage plus the corn bread. To make over the recipe, I was able to sauté the vegetables in just 1 tablespoon of butter using a nonstick skillet. I know this sounds completely radical, cutting the butter down from 9 [126 g] to 1 tablespoon [14 g], but the sausage in this dish and the garlic cloves drizzled with olive oil still add their share of fat and flavor to the stuffing. If you want to make a big batch for a holiday dinner, double the recipe.

1½ garlic bulbs

1½ teaspoons [7 g] olive oil

½ teaspoon [.5 g] dried thyme

Canola oil cooking spray

2½ cups [113 g] corn bread, crumbled (see the recipe for light corn bread on page 146)

1½ cups [279 g] cooked basmati rice (or similar), cold

1 tablespoon [14 g] butter

¾ cup carrots [96 g], cut into ¼-inch [6-mm] dice

½ large onion, cut into ¼-inch [6-mm] dice

¾ cups [90 g] diced celery (fibers removed)

¼ cup [37 g] finely chopped green bell pepper

6½ ounces [184 g] smoked chicken-and-apple sausage (or another less-fat sausage), fully cooked with casing removed

1 tablespoon [4 g] finely chopped fresh sage leaves

2 teaspoons [12 g] poultry seasoning

1 teaspoon [6 g] freshly ground black pepper, plus more to taste

¾ teaspoon [5 g] salt (optional)

1½ cups [360 g] low-sodium chicken broth

1. Preheat the oven to 375°F [190°C]. Remove the top quarter of the garlic bulbs and set the bulbs on a sheet of aluminum foil. Drizzle them with olive oil, sprinkle each bulb with the thyme, wrap the foil securely around the bulbs, and bake for 30 to 35 minutes.

2. Coat a 9 x 13-inch [23 x 33-cm] baking dish with the cooking spray and set aside. In a large bowl, combine the corn bread and rice and set aside.

3. In a large nonstick skillet, melt the butter over medium-high heat. Add the carrots and sauté for about 2 minutes. Add the onion and celery and sauté until the onion is tender (about 6 minutes). Add the bell pepper and sauté 1 minute longer. Stir the vegetable mixture into the corn bread and rice mixture.

4. With your hands, break the sausage into small chunks and add it to the corn bread mixture, along with the sage, poultry seasoning, black pepper, and salt (if desired). Drizzle the chicken broth over the top of the corn bread mixture and stir to blend (add a little more broth, if needed; the stuffing should be well moistened).

5. Squeeze the garlic cloves from the skins and mix them gently into the stuffing (keeping them whole as much as possible). Season with pepper, and salt to taste, if desired. Transfer the stuffing to the prepared baking dish and bake until the top is golden and the stuffing is heated through (45 minutes).

Note To reheat the stuffing, bring it to room temperature, cover, and bake at 350°F [180°C] for 20 minutes. Remove the cover and bake for about 10 minutes longer.

Nutritional Analyses (per serving)

	BEFORE	AFTER		BEFORE	AFTER
Calories	396	244	Cholesterol	50 mg	28 mg
Protein	10 g	9 g	Fiber	2.5 g	3 g
Carbohydrates	36 g	37 g	Sodium	749 mg	513 mg
Fat	24 g	6.5 g	% Calories from Fat	54	24
Saturated Fat	10.3 g	2.3 g	Omega-3 Fatty Acids	.3 g	.2 g
Monounsaturated Fat	10 g	2 g	Omega-6 Fatty Acids	1.7 g	1 g
Polyunsaturated Fat	2 g	1.2 g			

Horseradish Mashed Potatoes

Makes 6 servings

Flavored with a pinch of garlic and a dollop of horseradish, this version of mashed potatoes can be a welcome variation on the top comfort food mashed potatoes and gravy.

2 pounds [907 g] Yukon gold or russet potatoes, peeled and cut into 1-inch [24-mm] pieces

1 cup [242 g] fat-free half-and-half

1 teaspoon [3 g] minced or chopped garlic

2 tablespoons [30 g] prepared horseradish (bottled)

1 tablespoon [14 g] butter, cut into pieces (no- or low-trans margarine can be substituted)

Salt and black pepper to taste

1. Add the potatoes to a large pot of salted boiling water and boil until tender (about 20 minutes).

2. While the potatoes are boiling, add the half-and-half and garlic to a medium-sized nonstick saucepan and bring to a gentle boil. Stir in the horseradish and turn off the heat. Cover to keep warm until needed.

3. Drain the potatoes well and transfer them to the bowl of an electric mixer.

4. Slowly pour the half-and-half mixture into the bowl with the potatoes and beat on low. Add the butter and beat until it is blended. Add salt and pepper to taste.

Nutritional Analyses (per serving)

	BEFORE	AFTER		BEFORE	AFTER
Calories	208	154	Cholesterol	35 mg	7 mg
Protein	5.5 g	7.5 g	Fiber	3 g	3 g
Carbohydrates	28 g	32 g	Sodium	287 mg	278 mg
Fat	10 g	2 g	% Calories from Fat	42	12
Saturated Fat	6 g	1.2 g	Omega-3 Fatty Acids	.1 g	.03 g
Monounsaturated Fat	3 g	.6 g	Omega-6 Fatty Acids	.1 g	.06 g
Polyunsaturated Fat	.2 g	.1 g			

CHAPTER SIX

Wake Up and Smell the Brunch

These wonderfully light and comforting brunch dishes—from fluffy buttermilk pancakes to classic crumb coffee cake—will give you a good reason to get up in the morning. Create a breakfast or brunch tradition in your house by making one of these favorite foods a regular weekend guest.

Brunch Enchiladas

Makes 8 servings

I've never had enchiladas for brunch, but after tasting this light version, I decided that it's never too late to start. These enchiladas are filled with extra-lean ham, some high-flavor vegetables, and reduced-fat Cheddar cheese, then baked in a creamy egg batter made with fat-free half-and-half, a few real eggs, and some egg substitute. This is one of those breakfast dishes you make the night before, so it's perfect for busy mornings.

¾ pound [340 g] extra-lean cooked ham, trimmed of any visible fat and finely chopped (turkey ham can be substituted)

¾ cup [75 g] sliced green onions

¾ cup [112 g] chopped red or green bell pepper

1 (4-ounce [113-g]) can diced green chilies

8 to 9 whole-wheat flour tortillas (7-inch [18-cm] size)

3 cups [339 g] shredded reduced-fat Cheddar cheese or a combination of half reduced-fat Monterey Jack and half reduced-fat Cheddar, divided

2½ cups [605 g] fat-free half-and-half

3 eggs, beaten

½ cup [126 g] egg substitute

1 tablespoon [8 g] all-purpose flour

¼ teaspoon [1 g] garlic powder

A couple of dashes hot pepper or Tabasco sauce

Fat-free sour cream, salsa, and avocado wedges (optional garnish)

1. Coat a 9 x 13-inch [23 x 33-cm] baking dish with aluminum foil and coat the foil with the cooking spray.

2. Place the ham, green onions, bell pepper, and chilies in a medium-sized bowl and toss to blend well.

3. Wrap the tortillas in a slightly damp kitchen towel and warm them in the microwave on high for about 20 seconds or so (the tortillas should be soft and bendable). Spoon ⅓ cup [94 g] of the ham mixture and 3 tablespoons [15 g] of the cheese down the center of each tortilla, then roll up. Carefully place the filled tortillas, seam side down, in the baking dish.

4. In the bowl of an electric mixer, beat together the half-and-half, eggs, egg substitute, flour, garlic powder, and hot pepper sauce. Pour this mixture evenly over the tortillas. Cover the baking dish and refrigerate overnight.

5. The next morning, preheat the oven to 350°F [180°C]. Bake the enchiladas, covered, for 25 to 30 minutes. Remove the cover and continue to cook for 25 to 30 minutes longer, or until set. Sprinkle the casserole with the remaining cheese and bake for about 3 minutes longer or until the cheese melts. Let the casserole rest for about 10 minutes before serving.

6. Garnish with sour cream, salsa, and avocado wedges, if desired.

Nutritional Analyses (per serving)

	BEFORE	AFTER		BEFORE	AFTER
Calories	653	361	Cholesterol	229 mg	125 mg
Protein	30 g	33 g	Fiber	3.4 g	6 g
Carbohydrates	46 g	34 g	Sodium	1,282 mg	1,214 mg
Fat	37 g	13 g	% Calories from Fat	51	32
Saturated Fat	18 g	7 g	Omega-3 Fatty Acids	.3 g	.1 g
Monounsaturated Fat	14 g	2 g	Omega-6 Fatty Acids	2.2 g	.5 g
Polyunsaturated Fat	3 g	.6 g			

Homestyle Buttermilk Pancakes

Makes 6 servings (3 pancakes each)

Homemade pancakes can be very comforting—whether you like them topped with fresh straw-berries and whipped cream, or with a pat of butter melting on top with pancake syrup.

2 cups [250 g] unbleached flour (replace half
   the amount with whole-wheat flour,
   if desired)
2 teaspoons [9 g] baking powder
1 teaspoon [5 g] baking soda
2 tablespoons [26 g] sugar
½ teaspoon [3 g] salt

2 cups [490 g] low-fat buttermilk
¼ cup [60 g] reduced-calorie pancake syrup
¼ cup [63 g] egg substitute
1 large egg, lightly beaten
2 tablespoons [28 g] canola oil
1 teaspoon [4 g] vanilla extract
   or vanilla powder

1. Combine the flour, baking powder, baking soda, sugar, and salt in a medium-sized bowl and blend with a whisk.

2. Combine the buttermilk, pancake syrup, egg substitute, egg, oil, and vanilla in the bowl of an electric mixer and beat on medium-low speed just until smooth. Do not overmix.

3. Let the batter rest for 10 minutes. Preheat a nonstick skillet or griddle until hot.

4. Pour the batter by ¼ cupfuls [59 ml] onto the griddle. Cook over medium heat until bubbles form in the pancake (30 to 60 seconds). Turn over the pancakes with a spatula and cook for another 30 to 60 seconds, or until golden brown. Repeat this step until all the batter is used. Serve with pancake syrup or fruit and whipped cream.

Nutritional Analyses (per serving)

	BEFORE	AFTER		BEFORE	AFTER
Calories	372	289	Cholesterol	106 mg	40 mg
Protein	10 g	10 g	Fiber	0 g	0 g
Carbohydrates	51 g	46 g	Sodium	760 mg	670 mg
Fat	15 g	6.8 g	% Calories from Fat	35	21
Saturated Fat	8 g	1.1 g	Omega-3 Fatty Acids	.2 g	.5 g
Monounsaturated Fat	4 g	3.2 g	Omega-6 Fatty Acids	.5 g	1 g
Polyunsaturated Fat	.9 g	1.5 g			

Mexican Quiche

Makes 8 servings

It's important to have a breakfast that isn't too high in refined carbohydrates and is balanced with some protein and fat. This brunch dish fits the bill.

Canola oil cooking spray
5 eggs
½ cup [63 g] unbleached white flour
1 teaspoon [5 g] baking powder
Dash of salt
1¼ cups [314 g] egg substitute
½ cup [121 g] fat-free half-and-half or low-fat milk

2 cups [452 g] low-fat (low-sodium) cottage cheese, whipped in a food processor until smooth
8 ounces [227 g] mild green chilies, chopped
1½ cups [170 g] reduced-fat Monterey Jack cheese, shredded
1½ cups [170 g] reduced-fat sharp Cheddar cheese, shredded
Salsa, if desired

1. Preheat the oven to 400°F [200°C]. Coat a large casserole dish (or 9 x 13-inch [23 x 33-cm] baking dish) with the cooking spray and set aside.

2. In a large mixing bowl, combine the eggs, flour, baking powder, and salt and beat until well blended. Add the egg substitute and half-and-half and beat until smooth. Stir in the cottage cheese, green chilies, and cheese.

3. Pour into the prepared dish and bake for 15 minutes. Reduce the temperature to 350°F [180°C] and bake for 30 minutes longer. Serve with your favorite salsa.

Nutritional Analyses (per serving)

	BEFORE	AFTER		BEFORE	AFTER
Calories	372	282	Cholesterol	323 mg	166 mg
Protein	28 g	28 g	Fiber	1.3 g	1.3 g
Carbohydrates	11 g	13.5 g	Sodium	633 mg	576 mg
Fat	24 g	12 g	% Calories from Fat	58	41
Saturated Fat	13 g	7 g	Omega-3 Fatty Acids	.2 g	.1 g
Monounsaturated Fat	7.5 g	1.5 g	Omega-6 Fatty Acids	1.1 g	.4 g
Polyunsaturated Fat	1.3 g	.5 g			

Christmas-Breakfast Sausage Casserole

Makes 6 large servings

Almost every breakfast food group is represented in this recipe: sausage, eggs, milk, bread, and cheese. The only thing missing is some fresh fruit and a cup of coffee. Instead of the ground-pork sausage called for in the original recipe, I used a 50%-less-fat sausage and used less of it. I could see how the original recipe might seem greasy, with all that sausage. But because we cut extra fat wherever possible, the light version wasn't greasy at all—just yummy.

8 to 10 ounces [227 to 284 g] reduced-fat turkey breakfast sausage or 50%-less-fat sausage

Canola oil cooking spray

1 teaspoon [6 g] poultry seasoning

4½ cups [158 g] sourdough bread cubes, toasted (toast about 6 large slices and cut them into ¾-inch [19-mm] squares; other types of bread can also be used)

1½ cups (6 ounces [170 g]) shredded reduced-fat sharp Cheddar cheese

1 teaspoon [6 g] mustard powder

½ teaspoon [3 g] salt (optional)

2 large eggs

4 egg whites or ½ cup [126 g] egg substitute

2 cups [488 g] low-fat milk

1. Crumble the sausage into a medium-sized nonstick skillet. Cook over medium heat until nicely browned, breaking the sausage into bits as it cooks. Coat a 9 x 13-inch [23 x 33-cm] baking dish with the cooking spray and set aside.

2. Add the sausage to a large bowl along with the poultry seasoning, bread cubes, Cheddar, mustard powder, and salt (if desired).

3. Combine the eggs, egg whites, and milk in the bowl of an electric mixer and beat on medium-low speed until smooth and completely blended. Drizzle the egg mixture over the sausage and bread mixture and stir to blend. Pour into the prepared baking dish, spread the top evenly, cover with aluminum foil, and chill in the refrigerator for 8 hours or overnight.

4. Preheat the oven to 350°F [180°C]. Bake the casserole, covered, for 45 minutes. Uncover the dish, reduce the temperature to 325°F [170°C], and bake for about 20 minutes longer, or until set.

Nutritional Analyses (per serving)

	BEFORE	AFTER		BEFORE	AFTER
Calories	752	510	Cholesterol	231 mg	126 mg
Protein	31 g	31 g	Fiber	3 g	3 g
Carbohydrates	55 g	55 g	Sodium	1,280 mg	1,185 mg
Fat	44 g	15 g	% Calories from Fat	53	27
Saturated Fat	20 g	7.7 g	Omega-3 Fatty Acids	.7 g	.2 g
Monounsaturated Fat	17.5 g	4.4 g	Omega-6 Fatty Acids	3.8 g	2.4 g
Polyunsaturated Fat	4.5 g	2.5 g			

Cinnamon Crumb Coffee Cake

Makes 12 large servings

After about five different attempts, I finally created a lower-fat coffee cake that comes darn close to any crumb coffee cake you might get in a bakery. Among several changes, I used a combination of canola margarine or butter and light corn syrup instead of butter in the cake batter.

CAKE BATTER

½ cup [164 g] light corn syrup

⅓ cup [75 g] no- or low-trans margarine, softened

1 cup [200 g] sugar

1½ tablespoons [20 g] vanilla extract

2 eggs

2 egg whites

3 cups [411 g] cake flour

4½ teaspoons [21 g] baking powder

¾ teaspoon [5 g] salt

1½ cups [369 g] low-fat milk

CRUMB TOPPING

1½ cups [206 g] cake flour

1 cup [220 g] packed brown sugar

2 teaspoons [12 g] ground cinnamon

3 tablespoons [42 g] no- or low-trans margarine or butter, melted

1 tablespoon [15 g] reduced-calorie pancake syrup

Canola oil cooking spray

1. Preheat the oven to 375°F [190°C]. Lightly grease and flour a 9 x 13-inch [23 x 33 cm] baking pan using margarine, butter, or cooking spray.

2. To make the batter, cream the corn syrup and margarine with an electric mixer until smooth. Add the sugar, vanilla, eggs, and egg whites and beat until smooth and creamy.

3. Add the flour, baking powder, and salt to an 8-cup [2 l] measuring cup and stir to blend.

4. Add the dry ingredients to the creamed mixture, alternating with the milk. Beat with a mixer set on low just until blended. Pour into the prepared baking pan.

5. For the topping, combine the flour, brown sugar, and cinnamon in a small bowl and stir with a fork to blend. Melt the butter in a microwave using a small microwave-safe dish. Stir in the pancake syrup. Drizzle the melted butter mixture over the dry ingredients and stir with a fork to blend (it should form a dry, crumb mixture). Sprinkle this evenly over the top of the coffee cake batter. Spray the top with the cooking spray.

6. Bake for about 30 minutes, or until a fork inserted into the center comes out clean.

Nutritional Analyses (per serving)

	BEFORE	AFTER		BEFORE	AFTER
Calories	453	360	Cholesterol	98 mg	37 mg
Protein	6 g	6 g	Fiber	.7 g	.7 g
Carbohydrates	68 g	70 g	Sodium	488 mg	455 mg
Fat	18 g	6.5 g	% Calories from Fat	35	16
Saturated Fat	11 g	2 g	Omega-3 Fatty Acids	.3 g	.6 g
Monounsaturated Fat	5.2 g	2.4 g	Omega-6 Fatty Acids	.7 g	1 g
Polyunsaturated Fat	1 g	1.8 g			

Cranberry Upside-Down Coffee Cake

Makes 10 servings

This coffee cake is so delightful that it has become a weekend regular in my house. If you don't want to go to the trouble of inverting the coffee cake, just serve it straight from the pan (then the cranberry-pecan mixture will be on the bottom instead of the top).

Canola oil cooking spray
1½ cups [188 g] unbleached white flour
1½ teaspoons [7 g] baking powder
1 teaspoon [5 g] baking soda
½ teaspoon [3 g] ground cinnamon
¼ teaspoon [1 g] salt
⅓ cup [73 g] packed dark brown sugar
⅓ cup [79 g] reduced-calorie pancake syrup
3 tablespoons [42 g] butter (no- or low-trans margarine can be substituted)
2 cups [190 g] fresh whole cranberries

⅔ cup [72 g] chopped pecans
¼ cup [57 g] butter, at room temperature
¼ cup [60 g] fat-free or light cream cheese
¾ cup [150 g] granulated sugar
   (Splenda can be substituted, if desired)
¼ cup [63 g] egg substitute
1 large egg
1 teaspoon [4 g] vanilla extract
   or vanilla powder
⅔ cup [160 g] fat-free sour cream
⅓ cup [81 g] low-fat buttermilk

1. Preheat the oven to 350°F [180°C]. Wrap the outside of a 9-inch [23-cm] springform pan with aluminum foil (this protects your pan from leaking hot sugar). Coat the inside of the springform pan with the cooking spray.

2. Combine the flour, baking powder, baking soda, cinnamon, and salt in a medium-sized bowl. Stir the mixture well and set aside.

3. In a nonstick saucepan over medium heat, combine the brown sugar, pancake syrup, and butter. Bring to a complete boil and continue boiling for exactly 1 minute. Pour the mixture into the prepared pan. Sprinkle the cranberries and pecans evenly over this.

4. Combine the butter, cream cheese, and sugar in the bowl of an electric mixer and beat on medium speed until light and fluffy (a few minutes). Beat in the egg substitute and egg, one at a time, then stir in the vanilla. Beat in half of the flour mixture, then the sour cream, then the remaining half of the flour mixture, and then the buttermilk. Spoon the batter into the prepared pan.

5. Bake for 60 minutes, or until a toothpick inserted into the center of the cake comes out clean. Cool for 10 minutes, remove the sides of the pan, invert onto a serving platter, and carefully remove the bottom of the pan (which is now on top). Serve warm.

Nutritional Analyses (per serving)

	BEFORE	AFTER		BEFORE	AFTER
Calories	482	341	Cholesterol	99 mg	45 mg
Protein	5.5 g	6.5 g	Fiber	1.5 g	1.5 g
Carbohydrates	54 g	47 g	Sodium	466 mg	411 mg
Fat	28.5 g	14 g	% Calories from Fat	53	39
Saturated Fat	14 g	5.5 g	Omega-3 Fatty Acids	.4 g	.2 g
Monounsaturated Fat	10 g	6 g	Omega-6 Fatty Acids	2.3 g	1.9 g
Polyunsaturated Fat	3 g	2.1 g			

Caramelized Onion Tart

Makes 8 servings

Caramelizing onions requires a certain amount of fat, so you can't take it out of this recipe completely—just cut it down and switch to a no-trans margarine. This is no lean and healthful meal, granted, but these small adjustments make a huge difference and it still tastes terrific! If you are so inclined, you can make a crustless tart — just place the onions in a pie plate coated with canola oil cooking spray and then pour in the egg mixture and bake.

2 tablespoons [28 g] no- or low-trans margarine

4 cups [460 g] Maui or sweet onions, peeled, cut in half lengthwise, and sliced*

1 teaspoon [4 g] sugar (Splenda can be used, if desired)

½ cup [105 g] mashed potatoes (prepared or just mash 1 medium cooked potato without skin)

2 large eggs

½ cup [126 g] egg substitute

1 teaspoon [6 g] salt

¼ to ½ teaspoon [1 to 3 g] freshly ground black pepper

¼ teaspoon [1 g] ground nutmeg

1 cup plus 2 tablespoons [272 g] fat-free half-and-half

1 extra-deep 9-inch [23-cm] pie shell

1. Preheat the oven and a baking sheet to 375°F [190°C]. In a large nonstick skillet, melt the margarine over medium-high heat. Add the onions and sauté, stirring occasionally, until golden (about 5 minutes). Sprinkle with the sugar, stir, and sauté until nicely browned and caramelized (about 2 to 4 minutes longer). Remove from the heat and let cool.

2. Place the mashed potatoes in the bowl of an electric mixer along with the eggs, egg substitute, salt, pepper, and nutmeg and beat on low until smooth and blended. Slowly pour in the half-and-half while beating on low. Continue to beat on low until the mixture is well blended.

3. When the onions have cooled, spread them evenly in the bottom of the pie shell. Pour the egg and cream mixture into the pie shell. Place on the hot baking sheet in the center of the oven and bake until the crust is nicely browned and the center is set (about 45 minutes).

4. Remove the tart from the oven and cool slightly on a wire rack. Serve warm.

*Note If you use regular onions (not sweet), add 1 tablespoon [13 g] sugar toward the end of cooking the onions.

Nutritional Analyses (per serving)

	BEFORE	AFTER		BEFORE	AFTER
Calories	433	220	Cholesterol	198 mg	54 mg
Protein	7 g	8.5 g	Fiber	3 g	3.2 g
Carbohydrates	23 g	27 g	Sodium	562 mg	524 mg
Fat	36 g	8.5 g	% Calories from Fat	74	35
Saturated Fat	19 g	1.8 g	Omega-3 Fatty Acids	.5 g	.2 g
Monounsaturated Fat	11 g	3.5 g	Omega-6 Fatty Acids	2.9 g	2.1 g
Polyunsaturated Fat	3.4 g	2.8 g			

Overnight Crème Brûlée French Toast

Makes 6 servings

This is a wonderful cross between the elegant dessert crème brûlée and the breakfast favorite French toast. It can be very festive when you serve it with fresh berries and a dollop of light whipped cream. The savings between the original and this lightened recipe were huge. Calories went from 652 to 489, fat grams from 28 grams to 11, and the saturated fat went from 15 grams to 5. One of the best parts is that you can make this recipe the night before and just pop it in the oven the next morning.

Canola oil cooking spray

3 tablespoons [42 g] butter or
no- or low-trans margarine

5 tablespoons [75 g] reduced-calorie
pancake syrup

½ cup [110 g] packed brown sugar

2 tablespoons [30 g] Grand Marnier or other
orange liqueur

9 slices French or sourdough bread
(1-inch-thick [2.5-cm] each)

1½ cups [363 g] fat-free half-and-half

3 large eggs

½ cup [126 g] egg substitute

1 teaspoon [126 g] vanilla extract

¼ teaspoon [4 g] salt

Fresh strawberries or other berries and a
dollop or light whipped cream for garnish
(optional)

1. Coat a 9 x 13-inch [23 x 33-cm] baking dish with the cooking spray. Melt the butter in a small nonstick saucepan over medium heat. Mix in the pancake syrup, brown sugar, and Grand Marnier, stirring until the sugar is dissolved. Pour the mixture into the prepared baking dish.

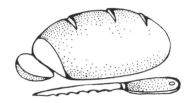

2. Remove the crusts from the bread and arrange the slices in the baking dish in a single layer on top of the brown sugar mixture. In a small bowl, whisk together the half-and-half, eggs, egg substitute, vanilla, and salt. Pour the mixture evenly over the bread. Cover well and chill for at least 8 hours or overnight.

3. Preheat the oven to 350°F [180°C]. Remove the dish from the refrigerator and bring to room temperature.

4. Bake, uncovered, for 35 to 40 minutes, or until the bread is puffed and lightly browned. Serve with fresh fruit and a dollop of light whipped cream, if desired.

Nutritional Analyses (per serving)

	BEFORE	AFTER		BEFORE	AFTER
Calories	652	489	Cholesterol	248 mg	124 mg
Protein	16 g	19 g	Fiber	3 g	3 g
Carbohydrates	80 g	76 g	Sodium	832 mg	796 mg
Fat	28 g	11 g	% Calories from Fat	39	21
Saturated Fat	15 g	5 g	Omega-3 Fatty Acids	.3 g	.2 g
Monounsaturated Fat	9 g	3.8 g	Omega-6 Fatty Acids	1.5 g	1 g
Polyunsaturated Fat	1.8 g	1.2 g			

Pecan Sticky Buns

Makes about 15 sticky buns

Skip the napkins and go straight for the moist towelettes after eating these treats! These sticky buns may be lighter than the ones you buy at bakeries and cafés, but they're still ooey, gooey, and delicious.

DOUGH
2 cups [250 g] unbleached white flour
2 cups [240 g] whole-wheat flour
1 cup plus 2 tablespoons [275 g] warm milk
    (105 to 110°F), low-fat or whole
¼ cup [63 g] egg substitute
½ cup [100 g] sugar
    (Splenda can be substituted)
3 tablespoons [42 g] canola oil
1 egg, lightly beaten
1 envelope active dry yeast
1 teaspoon [6 g] salt

TOPPING
¼ cup [60 g] no- or low-trans margarine
¼ cup [60 g] reduced-calorie pancake syrup
¼ cup [55 g] dark brown sugar
1 cup [99 g] pecan halves or chopped pecans

FILLING
2 tablespoons [28 g] no- or low-trans
    margarine
½ cup [110 g] packed dark brown sugar
2 teaspoons [12 g] cinnamon

1. Place the dough ingredients in a 2-pound [907-g] bread machine in the order recommended by the manufacturer. Set the machine on the dough cycle and press start. If you don't have a bread machine, combine the warm milk and sugar in a large bowl. Sprinkle the yeast over the mixture and let it stand until it gets foamy (about 6 minutes). Mix in the egg, egg substitute, oil, and the salt. Add enough flour, a cup at a time, to form a soft dough (about 4 cups [480 g]). Turn the dough out onto a floured work surface and knead until it is smooth and elastic, adding more flour if necessary to prevent the dough from sticking to your hands (about 10 minutes). Lightly oil another large bowl and place the dough in this bowl; turn the dough to coat the entire surface with oil. Cover the bowl with plastic wrap, then with a kitchen towel, and let it rise in a warm, draft-free area until it doubles in size (about 1 hour).

2. To make the topping, combine the margarine and pancake syrup in a glass measuring cup. Heat in the microwave for about a minute (or until the margarine is melted), stir together, and pour into a 9 x 13-inch [23 x 33-cm] baking pan. Sprinkle the brown sugar over the syrup mixture, then sprinkle evenly with the pecan halves; set aside.

3. When the dough is ready, roll it out on a lightly floured surface until it is about 19 inches [48 cm] long and 15 inches [38 cm] wide. It should be about ¼- inch [6 mm] thick.

4. For the filling, spread the margarine evenly over the surface of the dough. Combine the brown sugar and cinnamon in a small bowl and sprinkle the mixture evenly over the margarine-covered dough.

5. Working carefully from the 19-inch side [48-cm], roll the dough down to the bottom edge. Cut the rolled dough with a serrated knife into 1¼-inch-thick [30-mm] slices and place them in the prepared pan. You can cover the dough and leave it in the refrigerator to rise overnight or leave it at room temperature for an hour.

6. Bake the buns in a preheated 375°F [190°C] oven for about 20 minutes, or until they are light brown on top and cooked throughout.

Nutritional Analyses (per serving)

	BEFORE	AFTER		BEFORE	AFTER
Calories	378	296	Cholesterol	47 mg	15 mg
Protein	5.5 g	6 g	Fiber	1.5 g	3 g
Carbohydrates	45 g	44 g	Sodium	239 mg	242 mg
Fat	20 g	11 g	% Calories from Fat	47	33
Saturated Fat	6 g	1.7 g	Omega-3 Fatty Acids	.2 g	1 g
Monounsaturated Fat	7 g	6 g	Omega-6 Fatty Acids	5.8 g	2.2 g
Polyunsaturated Fat	6 g	3.3 g			

Apple Pancakes with Raspberry Sauce

Makes 6 servings

This is a light version of the special pancakes served at the Ahwahnee Hotel in Yosemite. This version uses less sugar and a lot less butter. Not only do the pancakes taste delicious but they look beautiful, too.

2 cups [250 g] unbleached white flour

⅓ cup [66 g] sugar, divided

1½ teaspoons [7 g] baking powder

¾ teaspoon [4 g] baking soda

½ teaspoon [3 g] salt

2 cups [490 g] low-fat buttermilk

¼ cup [63 g] egg substitute

1 large egg

2 tablespoons [30 g] reduced-calorie pancake syrup

1 tablespoon [14 g] canola oil

1 teaspoon [4 g] vanilla extract or vanilla powder

1 tablespoon [14 g] melted butter or no-trans margarine

3 large Granny Smith apples, peeled, halved, cored, and cut into ¼-inch-thick [6-mm] slices

¼ cup [62 g] apple juice

½ teaspoon [3 g] ground cinnamon

Canola oil cooking spray

½ cup [112 g] less-sugar raspberry jam or preserves

1. Preheat the oven to 250°F [130°C]. Blend the flour, 3 tablespoons [38 g] of the sugar, the baking powder, baking soda, and salt in a large bowl.

2. Whisk the buttermilk, egg substitute, egg, pancake syrup, oil, and vanilla in a medium-sized bowl; whisk the mixture into the dry ingredients and set aside.

3. Heat the butter in a large nonstick skillet over medium heat. Add the apples, apple juice, cinnamon, and the remaining sugar; sauté until the apples are golden (about 6 minutes).

4. Start heating a 10-inch [25-cm] nonstick skillet over medium heat. Coat with the cooking spray. Pour ½ cup [118 ml] batter into the skillet, tilting to form a 7- or 8-inch-wide [18- or 20-cm] circle. Cook the pancake until it's lightly browned on the bottom (about 2 to 3 minutes). Turn the pancake and lightly brown the other side (about 2 minutes). Place one-sixth of the apple mixture on half of the pancake and fold the pancake in half. Slide the pancake into a baking dish; keep warm in the oven.

5. Repeat with the remaining batter and apple mixture, spraying the pan with additional cooking spray as necessary.

6. Add the raspberry preserves to a glass measuring cup and warm it in the microwave on high (about 1 minute). Top the pancakes with the warm sauce.

Nutritional Analyses (per serving)

	BEFORE	AFTER		BEFORE	AFTER
Calories	531	391	Cholesterol	101 mg	45 mg
Protein	10 g	10 g	Fiber	4.2 g	4.5 g
Carbohydrates	81 g	74 g	Sodium	672 mg	602 mg
Fat	19 g	6.5 g	% Calories from Fat	33	15
Saturated Fat	8 g	2.2 g	Omega-3 Fatty Acids	.2 g	.3 g
Monounsaturated Fat	5.2 g	2.4 g	Omega-6 Fatty Acids	4.5 g	.8 g
Polyunsaturated Fat	4.7 g	1.1 g			

Cashew–Chicken Salad Sandwiches

Makes 3 sandwiches

To make a homemade version of this flavorful sandwich, I used skinless roasted chicken breast meat from one of those rotisserie chickens you find at your local grocery store. I added finely chopped celery and green onion and cashew pieces to the chopped chicken. I made the dressing with mayonnaise and fat-free or light sour cream, plus seasonings.

2 cups [280 g] chopped skinless roasted chicken breast (from a store-bought rotisserie chicken)

⅓ cup [40 g] finely chopped celery

1 finely chopped green onion (optional)

¼ cup [34 g] cashew pieces

4 teaspoons [19 g] light mayonnaise

¼ cup [61 g] fat-free or light sour cream

¼ teaspoon [pinch] curry

¼ teaspoon [pinch] chicken-broth powder

6 slices whole grain bread (focaccia bread or large slices of sourdough or whole-grain bread or rolls can also be used)

Lettuce leaves and tomato slices, if desired

1. Combine the chicken, celery, green onion (if desired), and cashew pieces in a medium-sized bowl and toss well.

2. In a small bowl, blend the mayonnaise, sour cream, curry, and chicken-broth powder together; drizzle over the chicken mixture and blend well.

3. Serve the chicken salad on the bread of your choice, topped generously with lettuce leaves and tomato slices.

Nutritional Analyses (per serving)

	BEFORE	AFTER		BEFORE	AFTER
Calories	682	410	Cholesterol	97 mg	84 mg
Protein	32 g	37 g	Fiber	3 g	6 g
Carbohydrates	44 g	32 g	Sodium	607 mg	344 mg
Fat	43 g	13 g	% Calories from Fat	57	30
Saturated Fat	8 g	2.8 g	Omega-3 Fatty Acids	.2 g	.1 g
Monounsaturated Fat	10 g	5.3 g	Omega-6 Fatty Acids	4.1 g	1.8 g
Polyunsaturated Fat	5 g	1.9 g			

CHAPTER SEVEN

Bread Therapy

Hot bread from the oven—there's nothing quite like it. Some think that the act of baking in and of itself is comforting. But the tasty results from the oven can give you the same comforting feeling. From chocolate chip–banana muffins to cheesy garlic bread to Grandma's scones, try them all and find your absolute favorites!

Mocha Chocolate Chip–Banana Muffins

Makes 15 muffins

3 ripe bananas (about 3 cups [450 g] sliced)

¾ cup [150 g] granulated sugar

½ cup [100 g] Splenda
  (sugar can be substituted)

⅓ cup [79 g] no- or low-trans margarine

⅓ cup [78 g] brewed coffee (decaf works, too)

⅓ cup [79 g] fat-free or light cream cheese

1 large egg

1 teaspoon [4 g] vanilla extract or vanilla
  powder

1¼ cups [156 g] all-purpose flour

1 cup [120 g] whole-wheat flour

1 teaspoon [5 g] baking powder

1 teaspoon [5 g] baking soda

¼ teaspoon [1 g] salt

1 cup [168 g] semisweet chocolate chips
  (the mini size works great)

1. Preheat the oven to 350°F [180°C].

2. Blend the bananas, sugar, Splenda, margarine, coffee, cream cheese, egg, and vanilla in a
   food processor for 1 minute. Add the flours, baking powder, baking soda, and salt and
   blend just until the flour mixes in. Fold the chocolate chips in with a wooden spoon.

3. Spoon the mixture into 15 to 18 paper-lined muffin cups. Bake for 25 minutes, or until
   cooked throughout. Cool on wire racks before serving.

Nutritional Analyses (per serving)

	BEFORE	AFTER		BEFORE	AFTER
Calories	315	212	Cholesterol	47 mg	15 mg
Protein	3 g	4 g	Fiber	1.7 g	3 g
Carbohydrates	43 g	36 g	Sodium	279 mg	237 mg
Fat	16 g	6.5 g	% Calories from Fat	45	28
Saturated Fat	10 g	3 g	Omega-3 Fatty Acids	.2 g	.4 g
Monounsaturated Fat	5 g	2.4 g	Omega-6 Fatty Acids	.4 g	.5 g
Polyunsaturated Fat	.6 g	1 g			

Ham and Cheese Muffins

Makes 12 muffins

These savory biscuitlike muffins are delicious with brunch or later in the day with a bowl of soup. The original recipe called for ½ cup [112 g] of mayonnaise, but I used 3 tablespoons [42 g] of light mayonnaise and ⅓ cup [80 g] of fat-free sour cream instead. I've also substituted reduced-fat cheese and extra-lean ham for regular ham and Cheddar cheese.

Canola oil cooking spray
2 cups [250 g] self-rising flour*
½ teaspoon [2 g] baking soda
1⅛ cups [273 g] low-fat milk
3 tablespoons [42 g] light mayonnaise

¾ cup [100 g] finely chopped cooked extra-lean ham
½ cup [57 g] shredded reduced-fat sharp Cheddar cheese
⅓ cup [80 g] fat-free sour cream

1. Preheat the oven to 425°F [220°C]. Coat a muffin pan with the cooking spray or line with paper cups.

2. Combine the flour and baking soda in a large mixing bowl. Combine the remaining ingredients in a separate bowl and then stir into the dry ingredients just until moistened.

3. Fill the muffin cups evenly (at least two-thirds full). Bake until the muffins are done (about 16 minutes). You can freeze or refrigerate any leftover muffins.

* *Note* Instead of self-rising flour, you can substitute 1½ teaspoons [7 g] baking powder and ½ teaspoon [3 g] salt, adding enough flour to equal 2 cups [250 g] total.

Nutritional Analyses (per serving)

	BEFORE	AFTER		BEFORE	AFTER
Calories	189	129	Cholesterol	18 mg	11 mg
Protein	6 g	6 g	Fiber	.6 g	.6 g
Carbohydrates	17 g	18 g	Sodium	496 mg	472 mg
Fat	11 g	3.2 g	% Calories from Fat	51	22
Saturated Fat	3 g	1.2 g	Omega-3 Fatty Acids	.4 g	.1 g
Monounsaturated Fat	3.2 g	.6 g	Omega-6 Fatty Acids	4 g	.4 g
Polyunsaturated Fat	4.4 g	.5 g			

Sweet Corn Bread with Honey Butter

Makes 9 servings

My goal with this recipe was to maintain the fluffy texture and sweet taste of restaurant-style corn bread while cutting the fat and calories. I think I accomplished that with this version by making several adjustments. This corn bread tastes great by itself, but it's heavenly served with honey butter.

Canola oil cooking spray
¼ cup [57 g] no- or low-trans margarine
¼ cup [60 g] fat-free or light cream cheese
¼ cup [50 g] granulated sugar
¾ cup [94 g] unbleached white flour

¾ cup [92 g] stone-ground or yellow cornmeal
1 tablespoon [14 g] baking powder
¼ teaspoon [1 g] salt
1 large egg
¾ cup [183 g] low-fat milk

1. Preheat the oven to 425°F [220°C]. Coat a 9 x 9-inch [23 x 23-cm] baking dish with the cooking spray.

2. In a large mixing bowl, cream the margarine, cream cheese, and sugar together for about 6 minutes with a standing mixer. Meanwhile, in a medium bowl, stir together the flour, cornmeal, baking powder, and salt.

3. Once the butter mixture has been beaten for 6 minutes, beat in the egg. Add the dry ingredients to the butter-egg mixture alternately with the milk, beginning and ending with the dry ingredients. Beat just until nicely blended.

4. Pour the batter into the prepared baking dish and bake until browned lightly on top and a fork inserted into the center comes out clean (about 20 minutes). Serve with Honey Butter (recipe follows), if desired.

Nutritional Analyses (per serving)

	BEFORE	AFTER		BEFORE	AFTER
Calories	214	158	Cholesterol	54 mg	25 mg
Protein	4 g	5 g	Fiber	.9 g	.9 g
Carbohydrates	24 g	24 g	Sodium	318 mg	318 mg
Fat	12 g	4.5 g	% Calories from Fat	49	25
Saturated Fat	7 g	1.4 g	Omega-3 Fatty Acids	.2 g	.4 g
Monounsaturated Fat	3.5 g	1.7 g	Omega-6 Fatty Acids	.4 g	.7.g
Polyunsaturated Fat	.6 g	1.2 g			

Honey Butter
Makes 8 tablespoons [120 g]

¼ cup [57 g] no- or low-trans margarine   ¼ cup [85 g] honey

1. Combine the margarine and honey in the bowl of an electric mixer or in a small food processor. Beat on low speed or pulse to blend the ingredients well.

2. Serve immediately or add the mixture to a custard cup, cover well, and store in the refrigerator until needed (use within the week).

Nutritional Analyses (per serving)

	BEFORE	AFTER		BEFORE	AFTER
Calories	82	65	Cholesterol	15 mg	0 mg
Protein	.1 g	.3 g	Fiber	0 g	0 g
Carbohydrates	9 g	9 g	Sodium	58 mg	75 mg
Fat	6 g	3.7 g	% Calories from Fat	62	51
Saturated Fat	3.5 g	1.1 g	Omega-3 Fatty Acids	.08 g	.4 g
Monounsaturated Fat	1.6 g	1.5 g	Omega-6 Fatty Acids	.1 g	.6 g
Polyunsaturated Fat	.2 g	1.1 g			

Banana-Nut Bread

Makes 12 servings

I ended up making three different versions of this lightened recipe, one using all white flour, one using half whole-wheat and half white flour, and one using white flour plus ground flaxseed. Each worked well, but I've got to admit that the one with the white flour looked the best and had a perfect, fluffy texture. You can sprinkle the nuts over the top of the batter in the loaf pan before baking, instead of stirring them into the batter.

Canola oil cooking spray
1¼ cups [281 g] mashed ripe bananas
  (about 3 bananas)
1 cup [145 g] dark brown sugar
  (granulated sugar can be substituted)
2 cups [250 g] flour (1 cup [120 g]
  whole-wheat pastry flour can replace
  one of these cups)*
1 teaspoon [5 g] baking powder

½ teaspoon [3 g] salt
¼ cup [63 g] egg substitute
1 large egg
1 teaspoon [5 g] baking soda
¼ cup [57 g] no- or low-trans margarine
¼ cup [60 g] fat-free or light cream cheese
1 cup [100 g] walnut or pecan pieces
¾ cup [109 g] raisins (optional)
2 teaspoons [9 g] vanilla extract

1. Preheat the oven to 350°F [180°C] and coat three mini loaf pans (6 x 3½ inches [15 x 9 cm]) or one regular loaf pan with the cooking spray.

2. Combine the mashed bananas and sugar in the bowl of an electric mixer, stir, and let stand for 15 minutes.

3. Combine the flour, baking powder, and salt in a separate bowl and stir with a whisk to blend well.

4. In a small bowl, combine the egg substitute and egg and stir with a fork.

5. Dissolve the baking soda in a tablespoon of warm water in a cup.

6. Add the margarine and cream cheese to the mashed banana mixture and beat until well blended (2 to 3 minutes on medium speed).

7. Add the dry ingredients, egg mixture, baking soda mixture, walnuts, raisins (if desired), and vanilla, and beat on low just until blended.

8. Pour the batter into the pan(s) and bake until a toothpick inserted into the center comes out clean (about 35 minutes for the mini loaves and 50 to 60 minutes for the large loaf).

Note If you use half whole-wheat flour, the fiber will be about 1 gram higher per serving. If you replace 6 tablespoons [47 g] of the white flour with ground flaxseed, the fiber will increase by 1 gram per serving.

Nutritional Analyses (per serving with nuts)

	BEFORE	AFTER		BEFORE	AFTER
Calories	308	264	Cholesterol	56 mg	18 mg
Protein	4.5 g	5 g	Fiber	1.7 g	1.7 g
Carbohydrates	39 g	39 g	Sodium	330 mg	334 mg
Fat	16 g	10 g	% Calories from Fat	45	34
Saturated Fat	6 g	1.6 g	Omega-3 Fatty Acids	.1 g	1.3 g
Monounsaturated Fat	2.5 g	3.2 g	Omega-6 Fatty Acids	.3 g	1.9 g
Polyunsaturated Fat	.4 g	3.8 g			

Nutritional Analyses (per serving without nuts)

	AFTER		AFTER
Calories	193	Cholesterol	18 mg
Protein	4 g	Fiber	1 g
Carbohydrates	38 g	Sodium	334 mg
Fat	3 g	% Calories from Fat	15
Saturated Fat	1 g	Omega-3 Fatty Acids	.3 g
Monounsaturated Fat	1.2 g	Omega-6 Fatty Acids	.5 g
Polyunsaturated Fat	.8 g		

Waffled Ham and Cheese Sandwiches

Makes 4 sandwiches (about 2 servings)

This recipe requires a nonstick waffle iron. Although it will work with a Belgian waffle iron, it works best with a regular one. To make these sandwiches with all the comfort and a lot less fat and calories, use a butter-flavored or plain canola oil cooking spray to coat the bread, an extra-lean-ham, and reduced-fat or light cheese. To boost the fiber, use whole-wheat, whole-grain, or fiber-enriched bread.

8 slices firm whole-wheat or whole-grain bread

Butter or plain-flavored canola oil cooking spray

2 ounces [57 g] extra-lean honey ham (or other type of extra-lean ham), thinly sliced

2 ounces [57 g] reduced-fat cheese of choice (such as Cheddar, Monterey Jack, or Jarlsberg Lite), thinly sliced or grated (about ½ cup, packed measure)

1. Preheat the waffle iron until it's hot.

2. Cut the crusts off the bread slices. Coat one side of the bread with the cooking spray.

3. Lay the bread, coated side down, on the bottom of the waffle iron. Top each slice with one-fourth of the ham and cheese, folding in any ham or cheese hanging over the edge of the bread. Top with the remaining bread slices, placing the coated sides up.

4. Cook the sandwiches until the bread is golden and crisp (about 2 to 4 minutes, depending on your waffle iron). Cut the sandwiches into two triangles and serve.

Nutritional Analyses (per serving)

	BEFORE	AFTER		BEFORE	AFTER
Calories	443	337	Cholesterol	66 mg	33 mg
Protein	19 g	19.5 g	Fiber	3.5 g	4 g
Carbohydrates	40 g	40 g	Sodium	959 mg	977 mg
Fat	22 g	9 g	% Calories from Fat	44	24
Saturated Fat	12 g	4.5 g	Omega-3 Fatty Acids	.2 g	.2 g
Monounsaturated Fat	6.3 g	1.7 g	Omega-6 Fatty Acids	.7 g	.7 g
Polyunsaturated Fat	.9 g	1 g			

Cheesy Garlic Bread

Makes 12 servings

I've been lightening various garlic bread recipes over the years, and this one is my favorite. It's a cross between garlic bread and cheese bread, and I use a little olive oil, no-trans margarine (with 8 to 9 grams of fat per tablespoon), and part-skim mozzarella. The spread keeps for days in the refrigerator, too.

1-pound loaf sourdough, French, or Italian bread

¼ cup [454 g] shredded part-skim or low-fat mozzarella cheese, packed

⅓ cup [80 g] no- or low-trans margarine

1½ tablespoons [21 g] extra-virgin olive oil

1 tablespoon [9 g] minced or chopped garlic

1 teaspoon [1 g] dried oregano

⅛ teaspoon [pinch] salt

Black pepper to taste

1. Preheat the broiler. Cut the loaf of bread in half lengthwise.

2. Combine the mozzarella, margarine, olive oil, garlic, oregano, salt, and pepper in a small food processor (an electric mixer will also work) and pulse briefly until you have a nice blended spread.

3. Spread the mixture on the bread halves, place on a jelly-roll pan, and broil for about 5 minutes, or until the bread is toasty brown (check often to make sure the bread doesn't burn). Cut into individual pieces and serve.

Nutritional Analyses (per serving)

	BEFORE	AFTER		BEFORE	AFTER
Calories	180	152	Cholesterol	23 mg	8 mg
Protein	4 g	4 g	Fiber	1 g	1 g
Carbohydrates	20 g	20 g	Sodium	343 mg	324 mg
Fat	9.5 g	6 g	% Calories from Fat	47	37
Saturated Fat	5.4 g	1.6 g	Omega-3 Fatty Acids	.1 g	.3 g
Monounsaturated Fat	2.9 g	3.1 g	Omega-6 Fatty Acids	.5 g	.7 g
Polyunsaturated Fat	.6 g	1.3 g			

Grandma's Scones

Makes 12 scones

To update this recipe, I still used butter (1 cup [227 g] was called for in the original recipe), but only half as much. In its place I added light cream cheese, which tends to work well in scones. I used fat-free in place of regular sour cream, and I kept the egg, but I used a higher omega-3 egg instead (you can use ¼ cup [63 g] egg substitute, if you prefer). The original recipe called for raisins or chocolate chips, but you can add any dried fruit you like (I tried dried cranberries).

Canola oil cooking spray
1 cup [242 g] fat-free sour cream
1 teaspoon [5 g] baking soda
2½ cups [313 g] unbleached white flour
1½ cups [180 g] whole-wheat flour
1 cup [200 g] granulated sugar (½ cup [100 g] Splenda can replace ½ cup [100 g] of the sugar, if desired)*
2 teaspoons [10 g] baking powder
1 teaspoon [6 g] salt

¼ teaspoon [1 g] cream of tartar
½ cup butter [114 g], chilled and cut into ¼-inch [6-mm] squares
½ cup [120 g] fat-free or light cream cheese
2 tablespoons [30 g] fat-free half-and-half
1 egg
¾ cup [109 g] fruit of your choice (dried cranberries, raisins, etc.) or ½ cup [84 g] mini chocolate chips
½ cup [84 g] white chocolate chips (optional)

1. Preheat the oven to 350°F [180°C]. Coat a large baking sheet with the cooking spray.

2. In a small bowl, blend the sour cream and baking soda and set aside.

3. Combine the flours, sugar, baking powder, salt, and cream of tartar in a food processor and pulse to blend well. Add the butter and cream cheese and pulse to cut in. (If you don't have a food processor, cut in the butter and cream cheese with a pastry blender.) Combine the flour and butter mixture in the bowl of an electric mixer, along with the sour cream mixture, half-and-half, and egg. Blend on low speed just until the dough forms. Fold in the dried fruits by hand.

4. Turn the dough out onto a lightly floured piece of wax paper and knead a couple of times. Roll or pat the dough into a ¾-inch-thick [19-mm] round. Cut this into 12 wedges and place them 2 inches [50 mm] apart on the prepared baking sheet.

5. Bake the scones for 15 to 20 minutes, or until they're golden brown on the bottom.

6. Decorate the scones, if desired, by drizzling them with white chocolate chips melted on low in a microwave. Serve warm.

*Note If you use ½ cup [100 g] Splenda, you will reduce the calories by 32 per serving and the carbs by 8.5 grams per serving.

Nutritional Analyses (per serving)

	BEFORE	AFTER		BEFORE	AFTER
Calories	438	345	Cholesterol	68 mg	41 mg
Protein	7 g	9 g	Fiber	.6 g	3 g
Carbohydrates	58 g	59 g	Sodium	539 mg	522 mg
Fat	21 g	9 g	% Calories from Fat	42	23
Saturated Fat	12 g	5.2 g	Omega-3 Fatty Acids	.3 g	.2 g
Monounsaturated Fat	6 g	2.4 g	Omega-6 Fatty Acids	.5 g	.35 g
Polyunsaturated Fat	.8 g	.6 g			

Challah Bread Braid

Makes 12 big slices

This moist, yellow bread is a traditional Jewish yeast bread that is often served on the Sabbath and other special occasions. It's yellow because the dough contains a couple of egg yolks and another egg yolk is brushed on top before it bakes. This is a lower-calorie, lower-fat, and lower-cholesterol version, and it tastes great fresh out of the oven or sliced days later and used to make French toast. I created this recipe using a bread machine—but only until you reach the point of the second rising (also known as the "dough" setting). Then you take the dough out of the machine, braid it, and let it rise once more before baking.

¾ cup [183 g] low-fat milk, warm to the touch (microwave on high for 30 to 50 seconds)

1 large egg, lightly beaten

¼ cup [63 g] egg substitute

2 tablespoons [28 g] butter or canola margarine

1 tablespoon [21 g] honey

3 cups [411 g] all-purpose or bread flour

¼ cup [50 g] granulated sugar

1½ teaspoons [9 g] salt

1½ teaspoons [6 g] active dry yeast (or 1 packet)

2 tablespoons [31 g] low-fat milk

1. Add the ingredients to the bread machine in the order suggested by the manufacturer. For my machine, I added the milk, then the egg and egg substitute, butter, honey, and then flour. I added the sugar on top of the flour, spooned the salt into one of the corners, and made a well in the center of the flour and added the yeast.

2. Select the dough cycle (about 1 hour and 40 minutes) and press start.

3. When the dough cycle is finished, preheat the oven to 375°F [190°C]. Then divide the dough into three equal parts. On a lightly floured work surface, roll each part into a rope about 16 inches long. Line the three ropes up, side by side, on a large cookie sheet. Press the ropes together at the top end and braid, pressing the ends together when you reach the bottom.

4. Brush the tops of the braids generously with the low-fat milk. Set the cookie sheet on top of the oven (or another warm place) and let the braids rise for about 30 minutes. Bake for 35 to 45 minutes, or until lightly browned.

Nutritional Analyses (per serving)

	BEFORE	AFTER		BEFORE	AFTER
Calories	178	156	Cholesterol	48 mg	24 mg
Protein	5 g	5 g	Fiber	.9 g	1 g
Carbohydrates	28 g	28 g	Sodium	348 mg	334 mg
Fat	5.5 g	2.5 g	% Calories from Fat	26	14
Saturated Fat	3 g	1.4 g	Omega-3 Fatty Acids	.1 g	.03 g
Monounsaturated Fat	1.6 g	.8 g	Omega-6 Fatty Acids	.2 g	.1 g
Polyunsaturated Fat	.3 g	.13 g			

Cranberry-Walnut Bread

Makes 12 slices

I love the texture and flavor of this bread. Some people prefer the tart cranberries, while others might want to toss their cranberries with a couple of tablespoons of sugar to add some sweetness before stirring them into the batter. When fresh cranberries aren't available, you can make the bread with dried cranberries.

Canola oil cooking spray
1 cup [200 g] sugar
½ cup [123 g] low-fat buttermilk
¼ cup [55 g] canola oil
¼ cup [63 g] egg substitute
1 egg
2 cups [250 g] unbleached white flour
1½ teaspoons [7 g] baking powder

¼ teaspoon [1 g] salt
¾ cup [186 g] orange juice
2 teaspoons [4 g] orange zest (add 1 teaspoon [2 g] more if you like a stronger orange flavor)
1 cup [95 g] cranberries or ⅔ cup [80 g] dried cranberries
½ cup [59 g] coarsely chopped walnuts*

1. Preheat the oven to 350°F [180°C]. Coat a 9 x 5-inch [23 x 13-cm] loaf pan with the cooking spray (or lightly grease and flour it).

2. Combine the sugar, buttermilk, and oil in the bowl of an electric mixer and beat until fully blended. Slowly beat in the egg substitute and egg.

3. In a separate mixing bowl, combine the flour, baking powder, and salt and slowly beat the dry mixture into the egg mixture. With the mixer on low speed, beat in the orange juice and orange zest.

4. Gently fold in the cranberries and walnuts. Pour the batter into the prepared pan.

5. Bake the bread for about 60 to 65 minutes (or until a toothpick inserted into the center comes out clean). Cool the pan for 10 minutes before inverting it onto a wire rack. Serve warm.

*Note If you omit the walnuts, each slice will contain 204 calories, 5 grams fat (.5 g saturated, 2.9 g monounsaturated, 1.5 g polyunsaturated), 18 mg cholesterol, 1 gram fiber, and 23 percent calories from fat.

Nutritional Analyses (per serving)

	BEFORE	AFTER		BEFORE	AFTER
Calories	287	229	Cholesterol	36 mg	18 mg
Protein	5.5 g	4.3 g	Fiber	1.3 g	1.2 g
Carbohydrates	35 g	35 g	Sodium	115 mg	125 mg
Fat	15 g	8.5 g	% Calories from Fat	46	33
Saturated Fat	1.3 g	1.2 g	Omega-3 Fatty Acids	1 g	9 g
Monounsaturated Fat	7 g	3.4 g	Omega-6 Fatty Acids	4.6 g	2.9 g
Polyunsaturated Fat	6 g	3.8 g			

Surprise Honey-Wheat Rolls

Makes 16 dinner rolls (or 2 medium-sized loaves)

This recipe requires a bread machine to make, but it's well worth the effort. The surprise is that the color and unique flavor of this bread come from two ingredients: cocoa and decaf coffee.

¼ cup [59 g] concentrated decaf coffee (espresso-strength)

1¼ cups [296 g] warm water

2 tablespoons [28 g] canola oil

⅓ cup [112 g] honey

2 cups [274 g] bread or unbleached white flour

1¾ cups [210 g] whole-wheat flour

1½ tablespoons [8 g] unsweetened cocoa

1 teaspoon [6 g] salt

1 package bread machine yeast (about 2¼ teaspoons [9 g])

Canola oil cooking spray

1. Add all the ingredients except the yeast and cooking spray to your bread machine in the order listed. Once everything has been added, make a well in the center of the flour and pour in the yeast.

2. Set the machine on the dough cycle (this normally takes around 1 hour and 40 minutes). When the buzzer goes off, shape the dough into 16 dinner rolls and let them rise on a baking sheet coated with cooking spray. If you are making two loaves, divide the dough in half and place each half in a loaf pan that has been coated with the cooking spray.

3. Let the rolls or loaves rise until they double in size (about 45 minutes). Preheat the oven to 350°F [180°C]. Bake until cooked throughout and browned on the outside (about 15 to 20 minutes for the rolls and 30 to 40 minutes for the loaves). Eat while they're still warm.

Nutritional Analyses (per serving)

	BEFORE	AFTER		BEFORE	AFTER
Calories	169	133	Cholesterol	0 mg	0 mg
Protein	4 g	4 g	Fiber	1 g	2.5 g
Carbohydrates	25 g	27 g	Sodium	146 mg	146 mg
Fat	6.5 g	2.1 g	% Calories from Fat	34	14
Saturated Fat	2 g	.2 g	Omega-3 Fatty Acids	.04 g	.2 g
Monounsaturated Fat	3.3 g	1.1 g	Omega-6 Fatty Acids	.9 g	.4 g
Polyunsaturated Fat	1 g	.6 g			

CHAPTER EIGHT

How Sweet It Is

For most women and some men, basically anything baked or sweet or made with chocolate is what defines a comforting dessert. Just in case this describes you, too, here's a chapter filled with light versions of the most comforting desserts you crave.

Black Forest Mini Cheesecakes

Makes 24 individual cheesecakes

You can't go wrong with mini cheesecakes! They're great finger food for a party, and they come with a guaranteed petite portion size. The original recipe called for vanilla wafers as the bottom crust. I used reduced-fat vanilla wafers to trim the fat and trans fats down as much as possible. I used light cream cheese for the filling, but if you prefer, you could bring this down one more notch by using one block of fat-free and one block of light cream cheese. With these and other modifications, I shaved off 50 calories and more than 8 grams of fat per mini cheesecake.

24 reduced-fat vanilla wafer cookies

2 (8-ounce [227-g]) packages light cream cheese

1¼ cups [250 g] granulated sugar

⅓ cup [29 g] unsweetened cocoa

2 tablespoons [16 g] all-purpose flour

¼ cup [63 g] egg substitute

2 eggs

1 cup (8 ounces [227 g]) fat-free or light sour cream

1 teaspoon [4 g] almond extract

TOPPING

1 cup (8 ounces [227 g]) fat-free or light sour cream

2 tablespoons [16 g] granulated sugar

1 teaspoon [4 g] vanilla extract

½ can (21 ounces [595 g]) cherry pie filling, chilled

1. Preheat the oven to 325°F [170°C]. Line muffin cups (2½ inches [6.5 cm] in diameter) with foil baking cups. Place one vanilla wafer, flat side down, in the bottom of each cup.

2. To make the filling, beat the cream cheese in the bowl of an electric mixer on medium speed until smooth. Add the sugar, cocoa, and flour, and blend well. Add the egg substitute and eggs, beating well after each addition. Stir in the sour cream and the almond extract. Fill each muffin cup three-fourths full with the batter.

3. Bake for 20 to 25 minutes, or until set. Remove the cheesecakes from the oven and let them cool for 5 to 10 minutes. While the cheesecakes are baking, make the topping by stirring together the sour cream, sugar, and vanilla in a small bowl until the sugar dissolves.

4. Spread a heaping teaspoon of the topping on each cheesecake. Cool completely on a wire rack; refrigerate. Just before serving, garnish each with a teaspoon of cherry pie filling. Cover and refrigerate leftover cheesecakes.

Nutritional Analyses (per serving)

	BEFORE	AFTER		BEFORE	AFTER
Calories	198	148	Cholesterol	58 mg	26 mg
Protein	3.5 g	4 g	Fiber	.4 g	.4 g
Carbohydrates	20 g	24 g	Sodium	90 mg	126 mg
Fat	12 g	3.7 g	% Calories from Fat	55	22
Saturated Fat	7 g	2.3 g	Omega-3 Fatty Acids	0 g	0 g
Monounsaturated Fat	3 g	.3 g	Omega-6 Fatty Acids	.5 g	.06 g
Polyunsaturated Fat	.6 g	.1 g			

One-Bowl Brownies

Makes 25 small brownies

This is a great recipe if you like your brownies on the cakey side. They are moist and full of chocolate flavor (because they're loaded with cocoa) but low in calories and saturated fat because canola oil (and not much of it) is used in place of butter.

Canola oil cooking spray

¾ cup [150 g] granulated sugar (if you don't want to use Splenda, make the granulated sugar 1½ cups [300 g] total)

¾ cup [150 g] Splenda

¼ cup [82 g] light corn syrup

⅓ cup [72 g] canola oil

⅓ cup plus 2 tablespoons [110 g] fat-free sour cream (light can be substituted)

2 teaspoons [8 g] vanilla extract or vanilla powder

¾ cup [65 g] unsweetened cocoa (sift the cocoa first)

½ cup [126 g] egg substitute

1 large egg

1 cup [125 g] unbleached white flour

½ teaspoon [2 g] baking powder

¼ teaspoon [1 g] salt

⅓ cup [39 g] chopped nuts (optional)

½ cup [84 g] chocolate chips, white, milk, or semisweet (optional)

Powdered sugar for dusting on top (optional)

1. Preheat the oven to 350°F [180°C]. Coat a 9-inch [23-cm] square baking pan with the cooking spray.

2. Add the sugar (and Splenda, if desired), corn syrup, oil, sour cream, and vanilla to a large mixing bowl and beat well by hand or with a mixer on low speed.

3. Add the cocoa, egg substitute, and egg and beat well after each addition until any lumps are gone.

4. Combine the flour, baking powder, and salt in a 2-cup [.5-1] measuring cup and blend briefly with a fork. Add the dry ingredients to the batter in the mixing bowl and mix by hand or with a mixer just until blended. Stir in the nuts and chocolate chips, if desired.

5. Pour the batter into the prepared pan. Bake in the center of the oven for 22 to 25 minutes, or until the brownies begin to pull away from the sides of the pan. Cool completely in the pan on a wire rack. Cut into bars.

6. Sprinkle the top with a little bit of powdered sugar, if desired.

Nutritional Analyses (per serving)

	BEFORE	AFTER		BEFORE	AFTER
Calories	160	92	Cholesterol	45 mg	9 mg
Protein	2 g	2 g	Fiber	.9 g	1.2 g
Carbohydrates	21 g	14 g	Sodium	102 mg	51 mg
Fat	8.5 g	3.5 g	% Calories from Fat	47	35
Saturated Fat	5 g	.5 g	Omega-3 Fatty Acids	.1 g	.3 g
Monounsaturated Fat	2.5 g	1.9 g	Omega-6 Fatty Acids	.3 g	.6 g
Polyunsaturated Fat	.4 g	.9 g			

Triple-Chocolate Decadence Cookies

Makes 24 cookies

This is one of my favorite chocolate cookie recipes. The cookies have the most amazing texture. I cut the butter in half and substituted chocolate syrup and strong coffee to replace the lost fat. I used egg substitute instead of two large eggs, and I reduced the amounts of chocolate chips and pecans a little, too, but they still taste heavenly.

½ cup [63 g] flour
½ teaspoon [2 g] baking powder
¼ teaspoon [1 g] salt
¾ cup [126 g] semisweet chocolate chips
2 ounces [57 g] unsweetened baking
   chocolate
3 tablespoons [42 g] butter
2 tablespoons [38 g] double-strength coffee
   (or espresso), cooled

1 tablespoon [20 g] chocolate syrup
⅔ cup [132 g] sugar
½ cup [126 g] egg substitute
2 teaspoons [9 g] vanilla extract
¾ cup [82 g] pecan pieces
   (toasted, if desired)
½ cup [84 g] white chocolate chips

1. Preheat the oven to 350°F [180°C]. Line two thick baking sheets or baking stones with parchment paper and set aside. (If you don't have parchment paper, spray baking sheets with canola cooking spray. It works, but the cookies tend to spread out more.)

2. Combine the flour, baking powder, and salt in a 2-cup [.5 l] measuring cup and stir to blend; set aside.

3. Place the chocolate chips, baking chocolate, butter, coffee, and chocolate syrup in a medium-sized microwave-safe bowl. Heat on high for 2 minutes and stir to blend and finish melting the chocolate. Heat for 30 seconds or longer if necessary to completely melt the chocolate. Set aside to cool.

4. Combine the sugar, egg substitute, and vanilla in the bowl of an electric mixer and beat on high speed for 2 minutes. Reduce to low speed and beat in the chocolate mixture just until combined.

5. Gently fold in the flour mixture with a rubber spatula, then stir in the pecans and white chocolate chips (the mixture will be very loose).

6. With a cookie scoop (or a small ice-cream scoop), scoop the mixture onto the prepared pans. Bake for about 8 minutes, until the surface of the cookie is dry (do not overcook). Let the cookies cool on the baking sheets, then peel them off the parchment. Store in an airtight container.

Nutritional Analyses (per serving)

	BEFORE	AFTER		BEFORE	AFTER
Calories	171	130	Cholesterol	26 mg	5 mg
Protein	2 g	2 g	Fiber	1.2 g	1 g
Carbohydrates	16 g	14.5 g	Sodium	73 mg	62 mg
Fat	12 g	8 g	% Calories from Fat	62	55
Saturated Fat	5.5 g	3.5 g	Omega-3 Fatty Acids	.05 g	.03 g
Monounsaturated Fat	2.6 g	1.7 g	Omega-6 Fatty Acids	.3 g	.15 g
Polyunsaturated Fat	.3 g	.2 g			

Peach Cobbler

Makes 12 servings

What could be better than peach cobbler hot from the oven, topped with a small scoop of light vanilla ice cream? You can use frozen peaches and have this old-fashioned dessert year-round.

Canola oil cooking spray

6 to 7 cups [1 to 1.2 kg] peaches, peeled, pitted, and sliced (32-ounce bag of frozen peaches)

¾ cup [150 g] granulated sugar, divided

¾ cup [150 g] Splenda, divided

1½ teaspoons [3 g] ground cinnamon

¼ cup [60 g] no- or low-trans margarine

¼ cup [60 g] fat-free or light cream cheese

¾ cup [94 g] unbleached white flour

¾ cup [90 g] whole-wheat flour

2 teaspoons [9 g] baking powder

½ teaspoon [3 g] salt

1 cup [242 g] fat-free half-and-half or low-fat milk

1. Preheat the oven to 350°F [180°C]. Coat a 9 x 13-inch [23 x 33-cm] or 10 x 10-inch [25 x 25-cm] baking dish with the cooking spray.

2. Combine the peach slices, 6 tablespoons [75 g] each of the sugar and Splenda, and the cinnamon in a large bowl and toss to blend; set aside.

3. In the bowl of an electric mixer, combine the remaining sugar and Splenda, the margarine, and cream cheese until the mixture is creamy and smooth. Add the flours, baking powder, and salt to an 8-cup [2 l] measuring cup and mix with a spoon to blend. Add the flour mixture to the margarine mixture alternately with the half-and-half. Pour the batter into the prepared pan. Top with the peach mixture, pressing the peaches gently into the batter.

4. Bake, uncovered, for 45 minutes, or until golden brown. Serve warm, topped with light vanilla ice cream, if desired.

Nutritional Analyses (per serving)

	BEFORE	AFTER		BEFORE	AFTER
Calories	305	191	Cholesterol	30 mg	1 mg
Protein	3 g	5 g	Fiber	2.6 g	3.5 g
Carbohydrates	53 g	40 g	Sodium	251 mg	248 mg
Fat	10 g	2 g	% Calories from Fat	29	9
Saturated Fat	6 g	.6 g	Omega-3 Fatty Acids	.1 g	0 g
Monounsaturated Fat	3 g	.8 g	Omega-6 Fatty Acids	.2 g	.1 g
Polyunsaturated Fat	.3 g	.6 g			

Earthquake Cake

Makes 20 servings

This cake reminds me of an upside-down German chocolate cake. The light rendition is super-moist and full of flavor.

Canola oil cooking spray

1 cup [77 g] flaked coconut (shredded unsweetened coconut can be substituted)

1 cup [117 g] finely chopped pecans or walnuts

1 (18¼-ounce [517-g]) box German chocolate cake mix or devil's food cake mix (with or without pudding in the mix)

1⅓ cups [315 g] water

¾ cup [182 g] fat-free sour cream, divided

½ cup [126 g] egg substitute

1 large egg

3 cups [360 g] powdered sugar

¾ cup [180 g] light cream cheese

3 tablespoons [42 g] melted butter (no- or low-trans margarine can be substituted)

1. Preheat the oven to 350°F [180°C] and make sure the rack is in the center of the oven. Coat a 9 x 13-inch [23 x 33-cm] baking pan with the cooking spray.

2. Scatter the coconut and pecans evenly on the bottom of the prepared pan.

3. Combine the cake mix, water, ½ cup [121 g] of the sour cream, the egg substitute, and egg in the bowl of an electric mixer and blend on low speed for 1 minute. Scrape the sides of the bowl with a rubber spatula and beat the batter for 2 minutes longer on medium speed. Pour the batter over the coconut and nuts and smooth it out with the rubber spatula.

4. Combine the powdered sugar, cream cheese, butter, and remaining sour cream in another mixing bowl. Beat on low speed for 1 minute, or until the mixture is smooth. With a large spoon, place globs of the cream cheese mixture on top of the cake batter. Distribute them evenly on top.

5. Bake the cake for about 45 minutes, but don't overbake because it will firm up as it cools down. Cool the cake in the pan on a wire rack for 30 minutes. Cut into squares and serve the cake upside down so the pecans and coconut are on top.

6. Cover the cake with aluminum foil and store it in the refrigerator for up to 1 week. This cake can also be frozen for up to 6 months. Just thaw it overnight in the refrigerator before serving.

Nutritional Analyses (per serving)

	BEFORE	AFTER		BEFORE	AFTER
Calories	359	290	Cholesterol	57 mg	27 mg
Protein	4 g	5 g	Fiber	1 g	1 g
Carbohydrates	40 g	41 g	Sodium	263 mg	277 mg
Fat	21 g	12 g	% Calories from Fat	53	38
Saturated Fat	7.5 g	5 g	Omega-3 Fatty Acids	.2 g	.1 g
Monounsaturated Fat	7 g	4.2 g	Omega-6 Fatty Acids	4.7 g	1.3 g
Polyunsaturated Fat	5 g	1.6 g			

Grandma's Old-Fashioned Sugar Cookies

Makes about 2 dozen cookies (possibly more, depending on the size of the cookies)

No one will ever know that these cookies have been lightened, since they have such great taste and texture. I've trimmed the fat in this recipe and switched to better fats by using no-trans margarine. If you don't want to use Splenda, just use ½ cup [100 g] granulated sugar and omit the Splenda. Add whatever decorations you want after baking; sugar crystals, red frosting, or raspberry jam work well.

Canola oil cooking spray

1½ cups [188 g] unbleached white flour

¾ teaspoon [3 g] baking powder

¼ teaspoon [1 g] salt

¼ cup [50 g] granulated sugar

¼ cup [50 g] Splenda (or substitute ¼ cup [50 g] sugar)

½ cup [120 g] no- or low-trans margarine

1½ tablespoons [23 g] fat-free half-and-half (plus more to brush on cookies, if desired)

2 tablespoons [31 g] egg substitute

½ teaspoon [2 g] vanilla extract or vanilla powder

½ teaspoon [2 g] almond extract

⅓ cup [74 g] sugar crystals (optional)

1. Preheat the oven to 400°F [200°C]. Coat the cookie sheet with the cooking spray.

2. Combine the flour, baking powder, salt, sugar, and Splenda (if desired) in the bowl of an electric mixer and beat on low speed to blend. Add the margarine and beat on low speed until the mixture resembles cornmeal (about 1 minute).

3. Add the half-and-half, egg substitute, vanilla and almond extracts all at once, then beat on low just until the dough forms. Chill the dough, if desired (it rolls out a little easier if it has been in the refrigerator for a few hours).

4. On a flat surface lightly coated with powdered sugar or flour, roll the dough out to ⅛-inch [3-mm] thickness. Cut into desired shapes with cookie cutters. Transfer the shapes to the prepared cookie sheet. Brush the tops of some of the cookies with half-and-half and sprinkle with sugar crystals, if desired.

5. Bake for 6 to 8 minutes, or until delicately browned.

Nutritional Analyses (per serving)

	BEFORE	AFTER		BEFORE	AFTER
Calories	86	54	Cholesterol	20 mg	0 mg
Protein	1 g	1.2 g	Fiber	0 g	0 g
Carbohydrates	10.5 g	8.5 g	Sodium	76 mg	74 mg
Fat	5 g	1.7 g	% Calories from Fat	46	29
Saturated Fat	2.6 g	.5 g	Omega-3 Fatty Acids	.06 g	.2 g
Monounsaturated Fat	1.3 g	.7 g	Omega-6 Fatty Acids	.1 g	.2 g
Polyunsaturated Fat	.2 g	.5 g			

Texas Sheet Cake

Makes 20 servings

You would be surprised at how popular this cake is in some regions of the United States. To lighten it, I've cut way back on the fat added to the batter and switched to a no-trans fat margarine. You can also use canola oil, but it lacks that buttery flavor. I decreased the amount of glaze made (don't worry, there's still plenty) and lowered the amount of fat normally used in the glaze, adding some coffee to make up the difference. I also replaced half of the white flour with whole-wheat pastry flour.

CAKE
Canola oil cooking spray
1 cup [120 g] whole-wheat pastry flour
1 cup [125 g] unbleached white flour
½ cup [100 g] granulated sugar
½ cup [100 g] Splenda (if you prefer not to use Splenda, increase the sugar to 1 cup [200 g])
¾ cup plus 2 tablespoons [195 g] coffee or water (depending on your preference)
⅔ cup [186 g] chocolate syrup
½ cup [112 g] no- or low-trans margarine (canola oil can be substituted)
¼ cup [22 g] unsweetened cocoa
½ cup [123 g] low-fat buttermilk
¼ cup [63 g] egg substitute
1 large egg
1 teaspoon [5 g] baking soda
1 teaspoon [4 g] vanilla extract or vanilla powder

GLAZE
¼ cup [22 g] unsweetened cocoa
6 tablespoons [92 g] fat-free half-and-half or low-fat milk
4 tablespoons [56 g] no-trans margarine
2 tablespoons [17 g] strong coffee (or increase the fat-free half-and-half by 2 tablespoons [17 g] if you don't want to use coffee)
4 cups [480 g] powdered sugar
½ teaspoon [2 g] vanilla extract

1. Preheat the oven to 400°F [200°C]. Coat a 10 x 15-inch [25.5 x 38-cm] jelly-roll pan with the cooking spray, then dust the pan lightly with flour.

2. Combine the flours and sugar (or Splenda and sugar) in the bowl of an electric mixer and beat on low speed until blended.

3. In a small nonstick saucepan over medium heat, bring the coffee, chocolate syrup, margarine, and cocoa to a boil, stirring frequently. Once the mixture comes to a boil, turn off the heat and pour it over the flour and sugar mixture. Add the buttermilk, egg substitute, egg, baking soda, and vanilla to the mixing bowl as well, and beat on low speed to blend everything.

4. Pour the batter into the prepared pan and bake in the center of the oven for about 20 minutes.

5. To make the glaze, combine the cocoa, half-and-half, margarine, and coffee in a small nonstick saucepan and bring to a boil. Remove from the heat and immediately stir in the powdered sugar and vanilla. Whisk the mixture until smooth, then immediately pour the glaze over the cake. Serve the cake warm or at room temperature. Cut the cake lengthwise into five columns and widthwise into four columns to make 20 servings.

Nutritional Analyses (per serving)

	BEFORE	AFTER		BEFORE	AFTER
Calories	369	228	Cholesterol	61 mg	11 mg
Protein	3.5 g	3.5 g	Fiber	1 g	2 g
Carbohydrates	57 g	47 g	Sodium	223 mg	150 mg
Fat	15 g	4 g	% Calories from Fat	37	15
Saturated Fat	9 g	1.3 g	Omega-3 Fatty Acids	.2 g	.3 g
Monounsaturated Fat	4.5 g	1.5 g	Omega-6 Fatty Acids	.4 g	.1 g
Polyunsaturated Fat	.6 g	1 g			

Applesauce Spice Cake with Vanilla and Spice Frosting

Makes 12 servings

I've lightened this recipe by using buttermilk instead of oil and fewer nuts. I used one token egg and substituted four egg whites, and this worked just fine. The cake tasted great!

Canola oil cooking spray

1 (18¼-ounce [517-g]) package Duncan Hines Moist Deluxe Spice Cake mix

1¼ cups [305 g] unsweetened applesauce

½ cup [123 g] low-fat buttermilk

4 large egg whites (or ½ cup [126 g] egg substitute)

1 large egg

Vanilla and Spice Frosting (recipe follows)

½ cup [55 g] chopped pecans or walnuts

1. Preheat the oven to 350°F [180°C]. Spray a 9 x 13-inch [23 x 33-cm] baking pan with the cooking spray, then lightly flour.

2. Combine the cake mix, applesauce, buttermilk, egg whites, and eggs in the bowl of an electric mixer and beat at medium speed for 2 minutes.

3. Pour the batter into the prepared pan and bake until a toothpick inserted into the center comes out clean (about 40 minutes). Cool completely.

4. Spread the frosting evenly over the cooled cake. Sprinkle with chopped nuts.

Nutritional Analyses (The "before" figures are per serving, without nuts and not including frosting. The "after" figures are per serving, without nuts and using Splenda.)

	BEFORE	AFTER		BEFORE	AFTER
Calories	327	211	Cholesterol	64 mg	29 mg
Protein	5 g	5 g	Fiber	1 g	1 g
Carbohydrates	36 g	36 g	Sodium	345 mg	364 mg
Fat	19 g	5.7 g	% Calories from Fat	53	24
Saturated Fat	4 g	2 g	Omega-3 Fatty Acids	.1 g	.1 g
Monounsaturated Fat	6.5 g	2 g	Omega-6 Fatty Acids	6.5 g	.1 g
Polyunsaturated Fat	6.8 g	.3 g			

Vanilla and Spice Frosting

Makes 12 servings of frosting (about 1½ cups [340 g])

3 cups [360 g] powdered sugar
½ cup [112 g] no- or low-trans margarine
1½ teaspoons [7 g] vanilla powder or
  vanilla extract

¼ teaspoon [1 g] ground cinnamon

1. Combine the powdered sugar, margarine, vanilla, and cinnamon in a small mixing bowl and beat on low speed until combined.

2. Increase the speed to medium and beat the frosting until it begins to have a whipped consistency (about 1 to 2 minutes).

Nutritional Analyses (per 2 tablespoons)

	BEFORE	AFTER		BEFORE	AFTER
Calories	165	146	Cholesterol	0 mg	0 mg
Protein	.4 g	0 g	Fiber	0 g	0 g
Carbohydrates	24 g	29 g	Sodium	69 mg	67 mg
Fat	7 g	3.3 g	% Calories from Fat	85	20
Saturated Fat	2 g	1 g	Omega-3 Fatty Acids	.1 g	.2 g
Monounsaturated Fat	3.4 g	1.3 g	Omega-6 Fatty Acids	.7 g	.8 g
Polyunsaturated Fat	.8 g	1 g			

Fudge-Truffle Cheesecake

Makes 16 servings

Two of my favorite foods are in this recipe title: truffles and cheesecake. I lightened the recipe all over, except when it came to the chocolate chips, since this is fudge-truffle cheesecake, after all! I even added Kahlúa liqueur to give a rich boost to the flavor of the cheesecake. You can turn this into raspberry-truffle cheesecake by adding a raspberry glaze over the top (warm ⅓ cup [74 g] to ½ cup [112 g] of seedless raspberry jam in the microwave on high for 1 minute).

Canola oil cooking spray

1 cup [80 g] (32 wafers) reduced-fat vanilla-wafer crumbs (use a food processor to puree into crumbs)

¼ cup [30 g] powdered sugar

3 tablespoons [16 g] unsweetened cocoa

2 tablespoons [28 g] melted no-trans margarine or butter

2 tablespoons [35 g] Kahlúa (strong coffee can also be used)

2 cups [336 g] semisweet chocolate chips (12 ounces)

2 (8-ounce [227-g]) packages light cream cheese

1 (8-ounce [227-g]) package fat-free cream cheese

1 (14-ounce [397-g]) can fat-free sweetened condensed milk

2 large eggs

½ cup [126 g] egg substitute

2 teaspoons [8 g] vanilla extract or vanilla powder

1. Preheat the oven to 300°F [150°C]. Coat the bottom and sides of a 9-inch [23-m] springform pan with the cooking spray.

2. Combine the vanilla crumbs, powdered sugar, and cocoa in the bowl of an electric mixer and beat on the lowest speed. Drizzle the melted margarine and Kahlúa over the top and beat on low until blended. Press the ingredients into the bottom of the prepared pan.

3. Place the chocolate chips in a 4-cup [1 l] glass measuring cup and heat in a microwave on high until the chocolate is melted and smooth (about 2 to 4 minutes), stirring after 2 minutes.

4. In the bowl of the electric mixer, beat the cream cheese on medium speed until fluffy. Gradually beat in the sweetened condensed milk until smooth. Mix in the melted chocolate, eggs, egg substitute, and vanilla. Beat on low speed until the ingredients are well blended. Pour the filling into the prepared crust.

5. Bake for 55 to 60 minutes. The cheesecake will seem underbaked in the center, but it will continue to cook after you remove it from the oven. Once it cools, keep it refrigerated until you're ready to serve it.

Nutritional Analyses (per serving)

	BEFORE	AFTER		BEFORE	AFTER
Calories	471	314	Cholesterol	124 mg	45 mg
Protein	8.5 g	10 g	Fiber	1.8 g	1.7 g
Carbohydrates	41 g	41 g	Sodium	270 mg	293 mg
Fat	33 g	13 g	% Calories from Fat	62	38
Saturated Fat	19 g	7.6 g	Omega-3 Fatty Acids	.4 g	.2 g
Monounsaturated Fat	10.5 g	3.1 g	Omega-6 Fatty Acids	1.2 g	.5 g
Polyunsaturated Fat	1.5 g	.7 g			

Perfect Peanut Butter Cookies

Makes 20 large cookies

This peanut butter cookie recipe is definitely the ticket to soft and fluffy cookies. I've lightened them up by replacing more than half of the butter with light cream cheese and fat-free half-and-half. I kept the brown sugar as is, but I replaced the granulated sugar with Splenda (you can stick with ½ cup [100 g] granulated sugar if you prefer). I used vanilla powder instead of vanilla extract and doubled the amount to deepen the flavor.

1 cup [258 g] smooth peanut butter

½ cup [100 g] Splenda (granulated sugar can be substituted)

½ cup [110 g] packed dark brown sugar

¼ cup [60 g] no-trans margarine, softened

¼ cup [60 g] light cream cheese

1 large egg (¼ cup [63 g] egg substitute can be used instead)

3 tablespoons [46 g] fat-free half-and-half or low-fat milk

2 teaspoons [5 g] vanilla powder or use 1 teaspoon [4 g] vanilla extract

1¼ cups [156 g] unbleached white flour

¾ teaspoon [3 g] baking powder

¼ teaspoon [1 g] salt

Canola oil cooking spray

1. Preheat the oven to 375°F [190°C].

2. Combine the peanut butter, Splenda, brown sugar, margarine, and cream cheese in the bowl of an electric mixer and beat on medium speed until well blended. Beat in the egg, half-and-half, and vanilla, one at a time. Beat on medium speed for about 1 minute to fluff up the batter.

3. Combine the flour, baking powder, and salt and beat into the creamed mixture on low speed just until combined.

4. Using a cookie scoop (⅛ cup [.03 l]), scoop the dough into balls and place them 2 inches [5 cm] apart on a cookie sheet that has been lightly coated with the cooking spray. Press each ball gently with the tines of a fork to flatten the cookie slightly and create a crisscross design on top.

5. Bake the cookies for 8 to 10 minutes in the center of the oven, or until the edges are lightly browned.

Nutritional Analyses (per serving)

	BEFORE	AFTER		BEFORE	AFTER
Calories	193	144	Cholesterol	24 mg	11 mg
Protein	5 g	5 g	Fiber	.8 g	1 g
Carbohydrates	20 g	15 g	Sodium	157 mg	148 mg
Fat	12 g	7 g	% Calories from Fat	54	49
Saturated Fat	4 g	1.6 g	Omega-3 Fatty Acids	.07 g	.0 g
Monounsaturated Fat	1.5 g	.5 g	Omega-6 Fatty Acids	.1 g	.03 g
Polyunsaturated Fat	.2 g	.3 g			

Mango Ice Cream

Makes about 1 quart of ice cream (or eight ½-cup [66-g] servings)

You need an ice-cream maker to make this exotic flavor. It delivers a good dose of fruit and a whole lot of rich flavor. Try it—you'll be surprised at how good it is.

½ cup [82 g] dried mango (optional)
½ cup [125 g] dark rum (optional)
1½ cups [248 g] frozen mango cubes or very ripe mangoes, peeled, seeded, and cubed
1¼ cups [303 g] fat-free half-and-half
6 tablespoons [78 g] sugar (Splenda can be substituted)

2 tablespoons [31 g] egg substitute
1 large egg yolk
½ cup [30 g] light Cool Whip (fat-free Cool Whip or light whipping cream can be substituted)

1. If desired, in a medium-sized bowl combine the dried mango with the rum; let the mixture soak for 2 hours, stirring after an hour. Drain the soaked mango (reserve the rum for another use) and dice it into ¼-inch [6-mm] pieces.

2. Place the mango in a food processor and pulse until a nice puree forms; set aside.

3. Add the half-and-half to a medium-sized nonstick saucepan and bring to a boil over medium-high heat. Meanwhile, combine the sugar, egg substitute, and egg yolk in the bowl of an electric mixer and beat with the whisk attachment on high speed until the mixture is pale yellow and fluffy (about 2 minutes).

4. Pour ½ cup [121 g] of the just-boiling half-and-half into the egg mixture and beat with the whisk attachment until well blended. Using a hand whisk, pour this new mixture into the saucepan with the remaining half-and-half and whisk until blended. Cook the mixture over medium heat until it is thick enough to coat the back of a wooden spoon (about 4 minutes).

5. Remove the creamy mixture from the heat and stir in the Cool Whip, rum-soaked mango, and the mango puree. Stir well to combine and let cool. Freeze in an ice-cream maker according to the manufacturer's instructions.

Nutritional Analyses (per serving)

	BEFORE	AFTER		BEFORE	AFTER
Calories	225	106	Cholesterol	114 mg	28 mg
Protein	2 g	4 g	Fiber	.6 g	.6 g
Carbohydrates	16 g	20 g	Sodium	19 mg	55 mg
Fat	18 g	1.3 g	% Calories from Fat	72	11
Saturated Fat	11 g	.8 g	Omega-3 Fatty Acids	.3 g	.02 g
Monounsaturated Fat	5.3 g	.3 g	Omega-6 Fatty Acids	.5 g	.1 g
Polyunsaturated Fat	.8 g	.1 g			

Easy Cocoa Ice Cream

Makes 6 cups (twelve ½-cup [66-g] servings)

Cocoa, fat-free sweetened condensed milk, and mostly fat-free half-and-half are combined in this eggless chocolate ice cream. You can add anything you want to this ice cream to make variations, such as miniature marshmallows and walnut pieces to create a light rocky-road flavor. Experiment to make your favorite flavor. You need an ice-cream maker to make this recipe.

1 (14-ounce [414-ml]) can fat-free sweetened condensed milk

⅓ cup [28 g] unsweetened cocoa

2 cups [484 g] fat-free half-and-half

1 cup [238 g] light whipping cream

1 tablespoon [3 g] vanilla powder or vanilla extract

1. In a medium-sized nonstick saucepan, combine the condensed milk and cocoa powder and stir. Cook over low heat, stirring constantly, until the mixture is smooth and slightly thickened (about 10 minutes). Remove the saucepan from the heat and let the mixture cool slightly.

2. Gradually stir in the half-and-half, light whipping cream, and vanilla, beating with a whisk until well blended. Refrigerate the mixture until it is cold.

3. Place the mixture in an ice-cream freezer container and freeze it according to the manufacturer's instructions for your particular ice-cream maker.

Nutritional Analyses (per serving)

	BEFORE	AFTER		BEFORE	AFTER
Calories	270	188	Cholesterol	115 mg	25 mg
Protein	5 g	7 g	Fiber	1 g	.8 g
Carbohydrates	22 g	27 g	Sodium	75 mg	91 mg
Fat	18 g	6.5 g	% Calories from Fat	60	32
Saturated Fat	10 g	4.1 g	Omega-3 Fatty Acids	N/A	.05 g
Monounsaturated Fat	7.5 g	2 g	Omega-6 Fatty Acids	N/A	.14 g
Polyunsaturated Fat	.5 g	.2 g			

Tapioca Pudding

Makes 6 servings

For those of you who grew up with tapioca pudding, this may be one of your favorite comfort foods. Here's a quick and light recipe that I hope you'll love. Try a version with dried cranberries and almond extract added for a fun variation on the traditional raisin and vanilla tapioca.

2¾ cups [671 g] low-fat milk
3 tablespoons [29 g] Minute tapioca
2 tablespoons [16 g] granulated sugar
2 tablespoons [16 g] Splenda
  (or substitute ¼ cup [50 g] sugar)

1 large egg
⅔ cup [109 g] raisins or currants
1 teaspoon [4 g] vanilla powder
  or vanilla extract

1. Whisk together the milk, tapioca, sugar, Splenda, and egg in a medium-sized nonstick saucepan. Let stand for 5 minutes.

2. Stir in the raisins. Cook, stirring over medium heat until the mixture comes to a full boil (it will take about 8 minutes). It will thicken as it cools. Remove it from the heat and stir in the vanilla. Allow the mixture to cool for 20 to 30 minutes.

3. Stir the mixture and spoon it into serving or dessert cups. Serve warm or chilled.

Nutritional Analyses (per serving)

	BEFORE	AFTER		BEFORE	AFTER
Calories	188	153	Cholesterol	50 mg	42 mg
Protein	5 g	6 g	Fiber	1.3 g	1.3 g
Carbohydrates	33 g	30 g	Sodium	70 mg	75 mg
Fat	5 g	2 g	% Calories from Fat	22	12
Saturated Fat	3 g	1 g	Omega-3 Fatty Acids	.07 g	.05 g
Monounsaturated Fat	1.5 g	.6 g	Omega-6 Fatty Acids	.02 g	.05 g
Polyunsaturated Fat	.3 g	.1 g			

Any-Fruit Crisp

Makes 6 servings

This is a wonderful fruit-crisp recipe that can incorporate whatever fruit is in season. I love fruit crisps and tend to experiment with all sorts of combinations, such as mango and boysenberry or apple and cranberry. This lower-calorie recipe seems to work well with just about any fruit combination.

CRISP TOPPING
½ cup [50 g] walnuts
1 cup [125 g] all-purpose flour
3 tablespoons [27 g] brown sugar
¼ teaspoon [1 g] ground cinnamon
Pinch of salt (if using unsalted butter)
3 tablespoons [42 g] melted butter
3 tablespoons [60 g] maple syrup, pancake syrup, or light pancake syrup

FILLING
4 cups [440 g] fruit, peeled and sliced, coarsely chopped, or cut into ½-inch [6-mm] dice
¼ cup [50 g] sugar
2 tablespoons [16 g] flour (if fruit seems particularly juicy, increase this by a tablespoon [8 g])

1. Preheat the oven to 375°F [190°C]. To make the topping, toast the walnuts by spreading them on a pie plate and heating until fragrant (about 7 minutes). Chop the nuts medium-fine.

2. Combine the flour, brown sugar, cinnamon, and salt (if using unsalted butter) in the bowl of an electric mixer. Drizzle the melted butter and maple syrup over the top and blend on low speed until crumbly. Add the chopped nuts and mix well. (The topping can be prepared up to a week ahead and refrigerated.)

3. For the filling, put the fruit in a large bowl. Add the sugar and taste, adding more if necessary. Sprinkle the flour over the fruit and mix gently. Spoon the mixture into a 2-quart [2 l] baking dish.

4. Spoon the topping over the fruit, pressing down lightly. Place the dish on a baking sheet to catch any overflow. Bake on the center rack of the oven until the topping is golden brown and the juices have thickened slightly (about 35 to 45 minutes).

5. Serve warm with light vanilla ice cream.

Nutritional Analyses (per serving)

	BEFORE	AFTER		BEFORE	AFTER
Calories	442	309	Cholesterol	41 mg	15 mg
Protein	4 g	4 g	Fiber	1 g	3.2 g
Carbohydrates	61 g	48 g	Sodium	162 mg	62 mg
Fat	22 g	12.5 g	% Calories from Fat	44	36
Saturated Fat	10 g	4.2 g	Omega-3 Fatty Acids	1.1 g	1 g
Monounsaturated Fat	5.3 g	2.6 g	Omega-6 Fatty Acids	4.2 g	4 g
Polyunsaturated Fat	5.4 g	5 g			

Creamy Cherry Pie

Makes 12 servings

Pies scored high in our comfort foods survey, so here's a light version of a popular recipe.

CRUST
Canola oil cooking spray
2 tablespoons [30 g] fat-free or light sour
   cream
1 tablespoon [14 g] melted butter or no-trans
   margarine
1 tablespoon [16 g] lemon or orange liqueur
   (Grand Marnier or Caravella)
1¼ cups [105 g] graham cracker crumbs
   (about 8 whole graham crackers; low-fat
   graham crackers can be substituted)

FILLING
1 (14-ounce [414-ml]) can fat-free
   sweetened condensed milk
1 cup [242 g] fat-free or light sour cream
¼ cup [61 g] lemon juice
1 (21-ounce [595-g]) can of cherry pie filling
   (a low-calorie version may be available)

1. Preheat the oven to 400°F [200°C]. To make the crust, coat the bottom and sides of a 9-inch [23-cm] deep-dish pie plate with the cooking spray.

2. Combine the sour cream, butter, liqueur, and graham cracker crumbs in a food processor and pulse briefly just until blended. (If you don't have a food processor, blend the sour cream, butter, and liqueur in a cup until smooth and drizzle the mixture over the graham cracker crumbs in a medium bowl, stirring well until completely blended.) Press the mixture into the bottom and partway up the sides of the prepared pie plate and set aside.

3. For the filling, combine the condensed milk, sour cream, and lemon juice in the bowl of an electric mixer and beat on low speed until smooth and creamy. Spread the mixture over the prepared crust.

4. Gently spoon the cherry pie filling over the cream mixture. Bake the pie for about 25 to 30 minutes, or until the filling appears to be set. Let it cool for about 30 minutes, then refrigerate to cool completely. Cut the pie into 12 wedges before serving.

Nutritional Analyses (per serving—the "after" figures are per serving, using regular-calorie pie filling)

	BEFORE	AFTER		BEFORE	AFTER
Calories	281	218	Cholesterol	30 mg	4 mg
Protein	4 g	5 g	Fiber	.6 g	.6 g
Carbohydrates	41 g	45 g	Sodium	153 mg	122 mg
Fat	12 g	1.7 g	% Calories from Fat	37	7
Saturated Fat	7 g	.5 g	Omega-3 Fatty Acids	.2 g	.03 g
Monounsaturated Fat	3.4 g	.5 g	Omega-6 Fatty Acids	.6 g	.3 g
Polyunsaturated Fat	.8 g	.5 g			

Key Lime Cheesecake

Makes 16 servings

This cheesecake is two desserts in one. If you like Key lime pie and you like cheesecake, you'll love this dessert. Top each slice with a dollop of light whipping cream and a slice of lime, if desired.

1 cup [84 g] low-fat honey graham cracker crumbs (about 6 whole graham crackers)

2 tablespoons [28 g] melted no-trans margarine or butter

1 tablespoon [21 g] honey

1 tablespoon [15 g] fat-free half-and-half or low-fat coconut milk

¼ teaspoon [1 g] coconut extract

24 ounces [680 g] light cream cheese, softened

½ cup [100 g] granulated sugar

½ cup [100 g] Splenda (granulated sugar can be increased to 1 cup [200 g] if you prefer not to use Splenda)

1 tablespoon [6 g] finely grated lime zest

4 teaspoons [11 g] cornstarch

2 eggs

¼ cup [63 g] egg substitute

⅔ cup [162 g] lime juice

1. Preheat the oven to 300°F [150°C]. Combine the graham cracker crumbs with the margarine, honey, half-and-half, and coconut extract. Press into the bottom of a 9-inch [23-cm] springform pan. Refrigerate.

2. In the bowl of an electric mixer, beat the cream cheese, sugar, Splenda, lime zest, and cornstarch until smooth and fluffy. Beat in the eggs and egg substitute, one at a time, blending just until smooth. Add the lime juice and mix on low. Do not overbeat or the cake will crack during baking. Pour the batter into the prepared crust.

3. Bake for 55 to 65 minutes, or until set. To minimize cracking, place a shallow pan half full of hot water on the lower rack during baking.

4. Turn the oven off and leave the cheesecake in the oven for 30 minutes with the door open at least 4 inches [10 cm]. Remove from the oven. Cover the cheesecake and refrigerate it overnight, or up to three days.

Nutritional Analyses (per serving—the "after" figures are per serving, using Splenda)

	BEFORE	AFTER		BEFORE	AFTER
Calories	268	178	Cholesterol	94 mg	46 mg
Protein	5 g	6 g	Fiber	.2 g	.4 g
Carbohydrates	21 g	18 g	Sodium	280 mg	261 mg
Fat	19 g	8 g	% Calories from Fat	48	40
Saturated Fat	11.5 g	5 g	Omega-3 Fatty Acids	.3 g	.1 g
Monounsaturated Fat	5.6 g	.5 g	Omega-6 Fatty Acids	.7 g	.1 g
Polyunsaturated Fat	1 g	.3 g			

Chocolate Lava Brownies

Makes 11 individual brownies

These brownies are heavenly, and quite possibly the best brownies I've eaten in a while. Make them using a cupcake pan, so that each serving is a beautiful, round mountain of chocolate waiting to be topped with a mini scoop of light vanilla ice cream, a dollop of espresso whipped cream, or a sprinkling of fresh raspberries.

8 ounces semisweet chocolate chips (1⅓ cups [223 g])

3 tablespoons [42 g] butter

⅓ cup [80 g] fat-free or light sour cream

1½ teaspoons [7 g] vanilla extract

½ cup [100 g] sugar

¼ cup [31 g] all-purpose flour

1 tablespoon [5 g] unsweetened cocoa

¼ teaspoon [1 g] salt

¾ cup [188 g] egg substitute

1 large egg

Canola oil cooking spray

Extra cocoa to dust muffin cups

1. Preheat the oven to 375°F [190°C]. Combine the chocolate chips and butter in a large glass measuring cup and microwave on high for a couple of minutes, stirring after each minute, until the chocolate has melted. (You can also melt the chips and butter in a double boiler over simmering water.) Stir in the sour cream and vanilla, and transfer to a large bowl.

2. In the bowl of an electric mixer, combine the sugar, flour, cocoa, and salt. Sift these into the chocolate mixture and blend well. Combine the egg substitute and egg and add to the mixture ¼ cup [63 g] at a time, fully incorporating each addition before adding the next. Beat on high speed until the batter is creamy and lightens in color (about 4 minutes). Refrigerate the mixture for about 30 minutes.

3. While the batter is chilling, lightly coat a 12-cup muffin pan with the cooking spray. Dust the cups with extra cocoa powder (about ¼ teaspoon [.5 g] per cup). Spoon the chilled batter into the prepared pan, using a ⅓-cup [.08 l] measure and filling each muffin cup almost to the top.

4. Bake for about 11 minutes—the outside should be cakelike and the center slightly gooey. Add whatever topping you desire and serve.

Nutritional Analyses (per serving)

	BEFORE	AFTER		BEFORE	AFTER
Calories	245	193	Cholesterol	100 mg	28 mg
Protein	4 g	4 g	Fiber	1.5 g	1.5 g
Carbohydrates	25 g	25 g	Sodium	162 mg	132 mg
Fat	16.5 g	9 g	% Calories from Fat	60	42
Saturated Fat	9.5 g	5.5 g	Omega-3 Fatty Acids	.2 g	.1 g
Monounsaturated Fat	5.2 g	3.1 g	Omega-6 Fatty Acids	.6 g	.3 g
Polyunsaturated Fat	.8 g	.4 g			

Bread Pudding

Makes 6 servings

Would you have guessed it? Pudding came up in our survey as one of the top comfort foods. One of the specific puddings mentioned was bread pudding. Here's a recipe for a lightened version of a bread pudding known to be served aboard Holland America's cruise ships.

Canola oil cooking spray
2 to 3 tablespoons [28 g] raisins
1⅛ cups [271 g] fat-free half-and-half
    or whole milk
1 tablespoon [14 g] butter or
    no- or low-trans margarine
1 vanilla bean, cut open lengthwise
½ teaspoon [2 g] vanilla powder or vanilla
    extract

¼ teaspoon [1 g] salt
6 tablespoons [94 g] egg substitute
1 large egg
⅓ cup [66 g] sugar
1 tablespoon [20 g] maple syrup
8 large but thin slices fiber-enriched
    white bread
½ teaspoon [1 g] ground cinnamon
2 tablespoons [16 g] powdered sugar

1. Preheat the oven to 350°F [180°C]. Coat a 9 x 5-inch [23 x 13-cm] loaf pan with canola cooking spray and set aside. Place the raisins in a small bowl, cover with water, and let soak for 10 minutes.

2. Combine the half-and-half, butter, vanilla bean, vanilla, and salt in a nonstick medium-sized saucepan and bring to a slow boil. Once the mixture boils, turn the burner off and let it cool for a few minutes.

3. Meanwhile, combine the egg substitute, egg, sugar, and maple syrup in the bowl of an electric mixer and beat on medium speed for about 1 minute. Remove the vanilla bean with a fork and slowly pour the milk mixture into the egg mixture.

4. Layer the bread slices in the prepared pan. Between each layer sprinkle some of the raisins (drained). Pour the milk mixture over the top. Place the loaf pan in a 9 x 13-inch [23 x 33-cm] baking dish filled with water about a third of the way up the sides of the dish. Bake the bread pudding until it's golden brown (about 30 to 35 minutes).

5. Combine the cinnamon and powdered sugar in a shaker and dust the top of the bread pudding generously with the mixture. Serve the pudding warm or cold.

Nutritional Analyses (per serving)

	BEFORE	AFTER		BEFORE	AFTER
Calories	353	206	Cholesterol	150 mg	37 mg
Protein	8 g	9 g	Fiber	1 g	3 g
Carbohydrates	43 g	36 g	Sodium	442 mg	338 mg
Fat	16 g	2.5 g	% Calories from Fat	41	11
Saturated Fat	9 g	.6 g	Omega-3 Fatty Acids	.2 g	.2 g
Monounsaturated Fat	5 g	.7 g	Omega-6 Fatty Acids	1.2 g	.1 g
Polyunsaturated Fat	1.4 g	.4 g			

Coconut Meringue Pie

Makes 12 servings

For those of you who have a hankering for a coconut *cream* pie, try to redirect your craving to a coconut *meringue* pie. It's not as heavy on the calories and fat, and it still tastes divine. Don't forget to let the egg whites sit out on the counter for about 30 minutes to bring them to room temperature prior to making the filling.

1 baked 9-inch [23-cm] pie crust

FILLING

3 cups [726 g] low-fat milk or
   fat-free half-and-half

½ cup [100 g] granulated sugar

½ cup [100 g] Splenda (or substitute 1 cup
   [200 g] sugar if you prefer not to use
   Splenda)

¼ cup [32 g] cornstarch

¼ teaspoon [1 g] salt

3 large egg yolks (reserve the whites for the
   meringue frosting)

1 tablespoon [14 g] no- or low-trans
   margarine or butter

1½ teaspoons [5 g] vanilla powder or vanilla
   extract

1⅓ cups [98 g] flaked coconut, sweetened
   and packaged

MERINGUE FROSTING

4 egg whites (three are reserved from the
   filling), at room temperature

¼ teaspoon [1 g] cream of tartar

¼ cup [50 g] granulated sugar

¼ cup [50 g] Splenda (or substitute
   ½ cup [100 g] sugar if you prefer not
   to use Splenda)

½ teaspoon [2 g] vanilla powder or extract

½ cup [37 g] flaked coconut, sweetened and
   packaged (optional)

1. Bake the pie crust (if you haven't already) just until lightly golden.

2. To make the filling, in a thick, medium-sized nonstick saucepan combine the milk, sugar, Splenda (if desired), cornstarch, and salt. Cook the mixture over medium to low heat, stirring constantly. After the mixture bubbles up and thickens, cook for another 2 minutes. Remove the pan from the heat.

3. In a medium-sized bowl, beat the egg yolks lightly. Gradually stir 1 cup [242 g] of the hot milk mixture into the yolks. Return the egg mixture to the saucepan and bring to a gentle boil. Cook, stirring 2 minutes more. Remove from the heat. Add the margarine and vanilla and stir until the margarine is melted.

4. Stir in the coconut and pour the mixture into the pie crust.

5. For the meringue, place the egg whites and cream of tartar in the bowl of an electric mixer and beat on high speed until foamy. Gradually add the sugar and Splenda (if desired), 1 tablespoon [5 g] at a time, until stiff peaks form and the sugar dissolves (about 2 to 4 minutes). Beat in the vanilla and spread the meringue over the hot filling, sealing to the edge of the pastry. Sprinkle the coconut on top of the meringue, if desired.

6. Bake at 350°F [180°C] for about 10 minutes, or until nicely browned. Cool the pie completely before cutting.

Nutritional Analyses (per serving)

	BEFORE	AFTER		BEFORE	AFTER
Calories	287	203	Cholesterol	85 mg	56 mg
Protein	5 g	5 g	Fiber	.5 g	.5 g
Carbohydrates	40 g	28 g	Sodium	231 mg	200 mg
Fat	13 g	8 g	% Calories from Fat	41	35
Saturated Fat	7 g	4.3 g	Omega-3 Fatty Acids	.1 g	.1 g
Monounsaturated Fat	3.6 g	2.5 g	Omega-6 Fatty Acids	.7 g	.6 g
Polyunsaturated Fat	1 g	.7 g			

Mini Pecan Pies

Makes 21 servings

The original version of this dessert is superrich because the filling is basically butter, brown sugar, and pecans—all encased in a fatty pie crust. One way to reduce the calories and fat grams in this treat is to eat a smaller serving size: This is a perfect recipe to make in miniature, so we'll be more likely to eat a small amount. I've also made some adjustments so that the recipe isn't quite as rich as regular pecan pie.

¾ cup [172 g] no- or low-trans margarine

1 (8-ounce [227-g]) package light cream cheese (nonfat cream cheese can be substituted)

2 cups [250 g] all-purpose flour

1¼ cups [275 g] packed dark brown sugar

1 large egg

2 tablespoons [47 g] egg substitute

1 tablespoon [14 g] melted no- or low-trans margarine or butter

1 teaspoon [4 g] vanilla extract

Pinch of salt

¾ cup [82 g] chopped pecans (increase to 1 cup [109 g], if desired)

1. Preheat the oven to 350°F [180°C]. You'll need two 12-cup muffin pans.

2. In a medium-sized bowl, combine the margarine and cream cheese and mix until well blended. Beat in the flour, ½ cup [63 g] at a time, just until the mixture forms a smooth dough. Knead with your hands to incorporate all of the crumbs at the bottom of the bowl.

3. Roll the dough into 21 balls and press each ball into the bottoms and sides of each muffin cup.

4. In another bowl, mix together the brown sugar, egg, egg substitute, margarine, vanilla, and salt. Stir in the pecans. Use a spoon to fill each of the crusts three-fourths full with the filling mixture (about 1 tablespoon [14 g]).

5. Bake for 15 to 18 minutes, or until the shells are lightly browned and the filling has puffed up. Cool, and carefully remove from the pans before serving.

Nutritional Analyses (per serving)

	BEFORE	AFTER		BEFORE	AFTER
Calories	240	170	Cholesterol	50 mg	15 mg
Protein	3 g	3 g	Fiber	.8 g	.7 g
Carbohydrates	24 g	22 g	Sodium	119 mg	119 mg
Fat	15 g	7.5 g	% Calories from Fat	57	40
Saturated Fat	7 g	2.4 g	Omega-3 Fatty Acids	.2 g	.4 g
Monounsaturated Fat	5.5 g	3 g	Omega-6 Fatty Acids	1.5 g	.9 g
Polyunsaturated Fat	1.7 g	1.8 g			

Caramel Apple Pie

Makes 10 slices

What would an all-American survey on comfort foods be without apple pie? This is a delicious crumb-topped apple pie with a caramel twist.

1 deep-dish prepared or homemade single
   pie crust

FILLING
6 cups [660 g] apples, peeled and thinly sliced
   (pippin or Granny Smith works well)
1 tablespoon [15 g] lemon juice
⅓ cup [66 g] Splenda (granulated sugar can
   be substituted)
2 tablespoons [16 g] unbleached white flour
¾ teaspoon [2 g] ground cinnamon
¼ teaspoon [1 g] salt
⅛ teaspoon [dash] ground nutmeg
6 tablespoons [114] caramel fudge sauce

CRUMB CRUST
½ cup [63 g] unbleached white flour
¼ cup [50 g] granulated sugar
¼ cup [50 g] Splenda (or substitute ½ cup
   [100 g] sugar if you prefer not to use
   Splenda)
½ teaspoon [1 g] ground cinnamon
¼ teaspoon [1 g] ground nutmeg
2 tablespoons [28 g] melted
   no- or low-trans margarine or butter

1. Set a cookie sheet or jelly-roll pan in the oven and preheat the oven to 375°F [190°C].

2. To make the filling, combine the apple slices and lemon juice in a large bowl. Add the Splenda, flour, cinnamon, salt, and nutmeg; mix lightly. Spoon this mixture into the pie crust, heaping it slightly toward the center. Drizzle the caramel sauce over the apple filling.

3. For the crumb crust, combine the flour, sugar, Splenda, cinnamon, and nutmeg in a medium-sized bowl. Drizzle the margarine over the top and blend with a fork until crumbly. Sprinkle the topping evenly over the pie filling.

4. To prevent overbrowning, cover the edge of the pie with aluminum foil. Set the pie plate on the cookie sheet or jelly-roll pan that has been preheating in the oven. Bake for 25 minutes. Remove the foil and bake for 20 minutes longer, or until the top is golden. Cool on a wire rack and serve.

Nutritional Analyses (per serving)

	BEFORE	AFTER		BEFORE	AFTER
Calories	329	194	Cholesterol	0 mg	0 mg
Protein	3 g	2 g	Fiber	1.7 g	2 g
Carbohydrates	46 g	36 g	Sodium	261 mg	204 mg
Fat	16 g	5.5 g	% Calories from Fat	43	26
Saturated Fat	4 g	1.7 g	Omega-3 Fatty Acids	.3 g	.3 g
Monounsaturated Fat	6.7 g	2.4 g	Omega-6 Fatty Acids	3.9 g	.5 g
Polyunsaturated Fat	4 g	.9 g			

20-Minute Tiramisù

Makes 16 servings

As I researched tiramisù recipes, I quickly discovered that there are literally hundreds of different versions out there. I took things I liked from several different recipes to create a version that I think is easier to make and delicious to eat!

SYRUP
½ cup [100 g] granulated sugar
½ cup [119 g] boiling water
½ cup [119 g] strong coffee
⅓ cup [79 g] Kahlúa

6 ounces [170 g] low-fat vanilla yogurt
1 teaspoon [4 g] vanilla extract
1 cup [238 g] heavy whipping cream

2 (3-ounce [85-g]) packages ladyfingers

FILLING
1½ cups [180 g] powdered sugar
¾ cup [180 g] light cream cheese
¼ cup [60 g] dark or light rum
⅓ cup [81 g] part-skim ricotta

TOPPING
⅛ cup [11 g] unsweetened cocoa for dusting
16 coffee beans to top each serving

1. To make the syrup, blend the syrup ingredients in a small saucepan and bring to a boil. Boil the mixture for about 5 minutes and set it aside.

2. To make the filling, combine the sugar, cream cheese, rum, ricotta, yogurt, and vanilla in the bowl of an electric mixer and beat on low speed to blend well, scraping the bottom and sides of the bowl. With the mixer on low, gradually pour in the whipping cream. Partially cover the bowl with plastic wrap (so that it doesn't splatter while it whips), increase the speed to medium-high, and beat until nicely thickened (about 2 to 2½ minutes).

3. To assemble, line the bottom and sides of a 9-inch [23-cm] springform or the bottom of a 9 x 13-inch [23 x 33-cm] pan with a layer of the ladyfingers. Drizzle 4 to 6 tablespoons of the syrup over the top. Spread half of the filling over the syrup-soaked ladyfingers. Cover with the remaining ladyfingers and drizzle about 6 to 8 tablespoons of the syrup over the top. Spread the remaining filling over the top and use a spatula to smooth.

4. Cover and refrigerate until you're ready to serve. Before serving, dust the top with cocoa (using a sifter or dusting cup) and top each serving with a coffee bean.

Nutritional Analyses (per serving)

	BEFORE	AFTER		BEFORE	AFTER
Calories	320	220	Cholesterol	80 mg	28 mg
Protein	3 g	3.5 g	Fiber	.2 g	.2 g
Carbohydrates	36 g	30 g	Sodium	140 mg	158 mg
Fat	17 g	8 g	% Calories from Fat	48	32
Saturated Fat	10.5 g	5 g	Omega-3 Fatty Acids	.2 g	0 g
Monounsaturated Fat	4.8 g	1.7 g	Omega-6 Fatty Acids	.5 g	.3 g
Polyunsaturated Fat	.7 g	.3 g			

Deluxe Banana Pudding

Makes 12 servings

I call this pudding "deluxe" because it's much more than just a pudding. It has several layers each of creamy pudding, vanilla wafers, and lemon-juice-soaked banana slices. Need I say more?

1 (14-ounce [414-ml]) can fat-free sweetened condensed milk

1½ cups [356 g] cold water

1 (3.4-ounce [96-g]) package instant vanilla pudding mix

4 cups [240 g] light Cool Whip

4 bananas, sliced

Juice of 2 lemons

About 36 reduced-fat vanilla wafers

1. In the bowl of an electric mixer, blend the condensed milk and water together. Sprinkle the pudding mix over the top and beat on medium speed for 2 minutes. Fold in the Cool Whip.

2. Dip the banana slices in the lemon juice and gently shake off the excess; place on a plate or in a shallow bowl.

3. In a 2½-quart [2.5-l] serving bowl (a see-through bowl works well), spoon one-third of the pudding evenly into the bottom of the serving bowl. Top with one-third of the banana slices and about 12 vanilla wafers. Repeat these layers two more times with the remaining pudding, banana slices, and wafers. Cover the bowl and chill until serving time. It will keep for up to two days in the refrigerator.

Nutritional Analyses (per serving)

	BEFORE	AFTER		BEFORE	AFTER
Calories	400	257	Cholesterol	66 mg	7 mg
Protein	5 g	4 g	Fiber	1.5 g	1.3 g
Carbohydrates	50 g	50 g	Sodium	232 mg	182 mg
Fat	21.5 g	4.4 g	% Calories from Fat	48	15
Saturated Fat	12 g	3.1 g	Omega-3 Fatty Acids	.3 g	.04 g
Monounsaturated Fat	7 g	.6 g	Omega-6 Fatty Acids	.9 g	.4 g
Polyunsaturated Fat	1.2 g	.4 g			

Index

Acknowledgments

Every now and then you are lucky enough to have a teacher that pours his heart and soul into teaching your child…a teacher that truly cares and can't help but inspire many of the bright-eyed students sitting in his classroom that year. Troy Spencer was one of those teachers, a 7th grade science teacher you hope and pray your next child will also get. In spite of radiation treatments through a large portion of the school year, this brave and very special man finished teaching his 7th grade students this year mere weeks before entering hospice. He took the time to write thank you notes to his T.A.'s, and to chaperone the end of the year field trip. He smiled when I wished him a wonderful and restful summer. I didn't know then that he had lost the fight against cancer. I didn't know.

What I do know is he is one of those special people you thank God are on this earth. I do know that he will be missed by my family and many others. I do know my daughter Devon's life is richer because she knew him. I do know he touched many and that he will never be forgotten.